Artwear

Melissa Leventon

Artwear
Fashion and Anti-fashion

With 197 illustrations, 185 in colour

Thames & Hudson

First published in the United Kingdom in 2005 by Thames & Hudson Ltd,
181A High Holborn, London WC1V 7QX

www.thamesandhudson.com

© 2005 Fine Arts Museums of San Francisco

Reprinted 2008

British Library Cataloguing-in-Publication Data
A catalogue record of this book is available from the British Library

ISBN 978-0-500-28537-4

Printed and bound in China

1·1 frontispiece

JANET LIPKIN American (b. 1948)
Nudes Coat, 1992
Loom-knitted wool

1·2 title page

K. LEE MANUEL American (1936–2003)
Conflicts/Contrasts, 1982
Painted leather and feathers, buttons

1·3 opposite

LIBERTY AND CO., LTD ARTISTIC AND
HISTORIC COSTUME STUDIO British
Day Dress (detail), ca. 1930
Raw silk pongee; smocked and embroidered
with silk

1·4 opposite

RANDALL DARWALL American (b. 1947)
Shawl (detail), 1989
Silk; dyed, handwoven in sixteen-shaft graded
twill weave

1·5 opposite

MARIO RIVOLI American (b. 1943)
Mexican Jacket (detail), 1989
Cotton, buttons, found objects; assemblage

1·6 opposite

MICHIKO KAWARABAYASHI Japanese
(b. 1942)
Shirt, Kite 1 (detail), 2000
Linen; hand-dyed

1·7 opposite

YVONNE PORCELLA American (b. 1936)
Diamonds on Ice (detail), 1984
Silk; painted, airbrushed, appliquéd, quilted

Contents

Acknowledgments

Countless people have helped me over the past five years as I have pursued the research and writing of this catalogue. Thanks must first go to Harry S. Parker III, Director of the Fine Arts Museums of San Francisco, who supported my work with the sabbatical and research stipend that allowed me to begin the project and subsequently agreed to undertake the exhibition, which gave me the context in which to finish it. Many members of the Museums' staff have helped with research or catalogue and exhibition production. I would like in particular to thank Trish Daly in the Textile Department; Sarah Gates, Joanne Hackett (formerly), and Beth Szuhay in Textile Conservation; photographer Joseph McDonald; technicians Robert Haycock and Virginia Benavidez; Sue Grinols, manager of Photo Services; Krista Davis, Director of Exhibitions, and Bill White, Exhibition Designer; Richard Sutherland and Allison Pennell, librarians; Therese Chen, Director of Registration, and Stephen Lockwood, Registrar; and Ann Heath Karlstrom, Director of Publications, assisted by Managing Editor Elisa Urbanelli and Suzy Peterson. Thanks are also due to Jennifer Minniti, California College of the Arts, for additional research.

My museum colleagues patiently answered questions and graciously made their collections and images thereof available. I'd like to thank Harold Koda, Lisa Faibish, and Charles Hansen, Costume Institute, the Metropolitan Museum of Art, New York; Anne Bissonnette, Kent State University Museum; Lynn Downey, Levi Strauss Archive; Sharon Takeda, Dale Gluckman, Sandra Rosenbaum, and Kaye Spilker, Los Angeles County Museum of Art; David Revere McFadden, Ursula Ilse-Neuman, and Linda Clous, Museum of Arts and Design, New York; Lauren Whitley, Museum of Fine Arts, Boston; Cindi Strauss, Museum of Fine Arts, Houston; Guus Boekhorst, Nederlands Textielmuseum; Inez Brooks-Myers and Suzanne Baizerman, Oakland Museum of California; Dilys Blum and Kristina Haugland, Philadelphia Art Museum; Gara Baldwin, Powerhouse Museum, Sydney; Bruce Pepich, Racine Art Museum; Melody Ennis, Rhode Island School of Design; Rebecca A. T. Stevens, The Textile Museum, Washington, D.C.; and Susan North and Sonnet Stanfill, Victoria & Albert Museum, London.

Galleries have been instrumental in tracking down objects and providing images; I am grateful to Julie Schafler Dale of Julie: Artisans' Gallery in New York; Helen Drutt English of Helen Drutt Gallery, Philadelphia; Jill Heppenheimer and Barbara Lanning of Santa Fe Weaving Gallery; Susie Hollingsworth of Wittenborn and Hollingsworth, formerly in Los Angeles; Keiko Kawashima of Gallery Gallery in Kyoto; Widney Moore of Widney Moore Gallery in Portland, Oregon; and Rudolf Smend of Galerie Smend in Cologne. I must also acknowledge the late Sandra Sakata of Obiko and the late Howard Steinman, who together introduced me to Kaisik Wong's work in 1991 and got me interested in the history of wearable art.

Dozens of artists took the time to talk to me, and to show me their work and provide me with images. There are too many to thank by name, but I am grateful to each and every one of them. I do want to name those artists, dealers, and collectors who took the time to sit for formal interviews: Gaza Bowen, Jean Williams Cacicedo, Marian Clayden, Marika Contompasis, Libby and Joanne Cooper, Julie Schafler Dale, Genevieve Dion, Tim Harding, Pat Henderson, Ana Lisa Hedstrom, Jill Heppenheimer and Barbara Lanning, Candace Kling, Fred Kling, Ina Kozel, Robert Kushner, Janet Lipkin, Nancy McNeil, K. Lee Manuel, Linda Mendelson, Famous Melissa, Marian Schoettle, Jo Ann Stabb, Susan Summa, Victoria Rabinowe, and Yoshiko Iwamoto Wada. In the Bay Area, several of the artists of Group 9—Cacicedo, Clayden, Hedstrom, Candace Kling, and Lipkin—stand out for the overwhelming generosity with which they shared their time, thoughts, contacts, feedback, and archives. Nancy Chappell and Yoshiko Wada also provided key assistance. I am grateful, too, to Diana Aurigemma, Lynn di Nino, and Mary Griffin of Friends of the Rag; Chunghie Lee; and Frances Butler and her partner Alistair Johnson. Several collectors also went out of their way to provide images or reference materials—in particular Bud Johns, Jeanne Rose, and Myrna Tatar.

Finally, to my family and friends, who showed amazing forbearance, understanding, and support during the long process of writing this book—Barb, Greg, Caia, FWI, Doug, Miriam, the study group, Candy—thank you. Most of all, to Scott, who has provided constant support (and my minimum daily requirement of horrible puns) while I did the research and wrote the book. I couldn't have done it without you.

This book is dedicated to my parents, Melvin and Eleanor Leventon.

Director's Foreword

Nowhere has contemporary American fiber art been more active and inventive than in the San Francisco Bay Area. Fiber artists have been drawn here by the light and the landscape, the unprecedented opportunities to study and exhibit, and the community of their fellows that has developed here. Through their work, the influence of the Bay Area has in turn spread outward to other parts of the United States and well beyond American shores. Artwear is one of the most distinctive features of contemporary fiber art and, while it is not unique to the Bay Area, it has been an integral part of the fiber scene here since the mid-1960s. Historically, the genre has been underrepresented in museums, though interest is now on the rise. The Fine Arts Museums, as pioneers in this field, acquired their first piece of wearable art in 1985 and are proud to have been collecting actively since the early 1990s.

Melissa Leventon has nurtured the Museums' artwear collection from its inception. She began work on this project during her tenure as the Fine Arts Museums' curator of textiles and, more recently, as guest curator, she organized the exhibition *Artwear: Fashion and Anti-fashion*, which accompanies and celebrates the publication of this book. In the book she has traced artwear's antecedent movements; its history in the United States, highlighting significant artists, galleries, and exhibitions; its characteristic forms and processes; its manifestations in other countries; and its important relationships to conceptual and performance art. The exhibition provides the occasion to look back at thirty-five years of wearable art, much of it created or collected in the Bay Area. It showcases thirty-five works from the Museums' holdings, many on view to the public for the first time. The book has also offered the opportunity to reproduce, also for the first time, many of these objects so painstakingly acquired by the Museums over the past fifteen years and to document this important portion of the textile collection.

Along with much that is new, the exhibition allows visitors to relive a bit of the Museums' past with the return to its galleries of part of Kaisik Wong's important *Seven Rays* series, last seen a decade ago, and several of the Levi Strauss Denim Contest winners, which were first shown at the M. H. de Young Memorial Museum in 1974. Although the exhibition has tremendous local strength it is, like the book, truly a global look at this phenomenon, boasting examples from across the United States, as well as from Britain, Europe, Australia, New Zealand, Japan, and Korea, and charting artwear's interactions with fine art and fashion as well as with fiber art.

The Museums are grateful to the many institutional and individual lenders, both here and abroad, who have been instrumental in bringing forth the exhibition. The early research for the catalogue was accomplished with support from the Museums, and we are delighted to have participated with Melissa Leventon in making this contribution to the public's knowledge of a fascinating genre.

Harry S. Parker III
Director of Museums

Introduction

Artwear, or wearable art, is a surprisingly difficult genre to pin down. It has gone by different names at different times in different places. It is a product of the postindustrial, Western battle of art versus craft, in which craft seeks validation as an equal to art and art seeks to maintain a proper distance. Yet it has also appeared in Asia, where the art/craft divide traditionally has not existed. Artwear struggles with an ever-changing relationship to fashion, which informs it and which it informs, but from which it has sought independence in its wish to achieve recognition as art. Its story over the past thirty-five years is one of shifting boundaries, as art, fashion, and wearable art maneuvered around and ultimately moved toward each other.

In its original form, *wearable art* denoted handmade textiles, created from traditional processes, which were then made into one-of-a-kind clothing by the textile artist (1.8). It was rooted both in art and studio fiber art and sought to define itself as separate from fashion by focusing on laborious techniques of fabric-making, by utilizing ethnic garment forms, and by emphasizing unique works made by a single hand, or sometimes by two or more artists in collaboration with each other, rather than multiples executed by artisans according to a designer's vision. Most of it is intended for formal or everyday wear, but it also has links to performance and conceptual art, and in these cases may or may not actually be wearable. The wearable art community thus conceived of and presented its output in terms of the formal trappings of the art world, and the importance of this framework should not be underestimated. By thinking of themselves as artists and not designers, by giving their works titles and subjects, even by insisting that their work, while functional, could also be non-functional, artists redefined the creation of clothing as art, not fashion. Further ammunition was provided by the conventions adopted by both artists and galleries for photographic presentation, which are far more akin to museum presentations than contemporary styles of fashion photography. They show artwear either as wall hangings or carefully positioned on a model in such a way as to offer maximum display of the textile—usually from the back—rather than the interaction of the garment with the body or the personality of the wearer (1.9). Yet at the same time that it sought to define itself as art, artwear also rejected the male-dominated art establishment and its contemporary movements like Minimalism. Many textile artists found little in these to interest them. They had a visceral attraction to their medium, were overwhelmingly female, and often wished to honor the women who introduced them in childhood to textile crafts. Theirs was nothing less than a bold attempt to create a home for themselves in art, where this particular aspect of "women's work" could finally take its rightful place.

In the hippie culture that was a springboard for wearable art on the West Coast of the United States, the idea that the wearer would know the maker personally, or simply know that the garment had been made by an individual rather than an industry, was also important, and the primacy of this personal connection between

1·8 opposite

ANA LISA HEDSTROM American (b. 1943)
Fan Vest, 1979
Shibori-dyed silk

Arashi (storm) shibori, a resist-dyeing technique invented in Japan in 1880, is the method Hedstrom used to dye the silk for this vest.

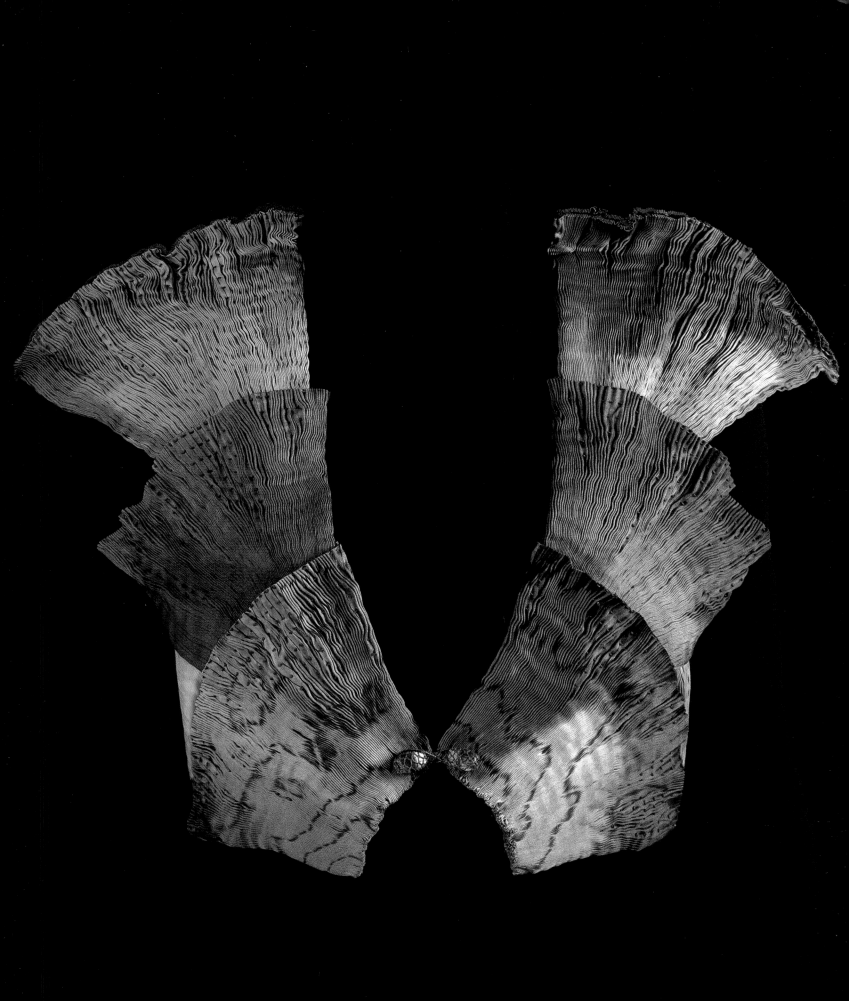

artist and patron blended with the genre's artistic and political aims. Even as artwear has evolved from those early goals, that sense of connection has continued to give it relevance and an aura of luxury in our increasingly mechanized and technology-saturated world. Wearable art's patrons include wearers of designer fashion, accustomed to picturing the individual behind the label, and a substantial population of middle-class women who may see these clothes as a proclamation that they are individuals of resources and iconoclastic taste, who understand and appreciate art and culture. The idea of connection is also important among the artists themselves, where it is based on shared values, aesthetics, and skills, and, perhaps, on the nature of creativity rooted in these specific, exacting physical processes. Artist networks, most of which arose in the 1980s and 90s, have helped give this increasingly diverse genre an identity, from local networks like northern California's Group 9, to those like the World Shibori Network, the European Textile Network, and the International Felt Society, which attract artists from all over the world.

Artwear has evolved considerably from its early form into today's multifaceted, international field that encompasses both wearable and unwearable garments and extends from studio fiber art to performance art and spectacle, to conceptual art, and, inevitably, back to fashion. The move back toward fashion began in the late 1970s and accelerated through the 80s as the folksy styles of the previous decade gave way to works that were smoother, more sophisticated, and less obviously handmade. Artists who stayed with the genre increasingly shifted from one-of-a-kind works produced alone or in small collaborations to a scenario in which they essentially became designers in charge of small fashion houses producing limited-edition works from handmade textiles. These fabrics are usually created in-house but may also be made to order by an outside concern. As artists have become more comfortable with the idea of working within the fashion system, they have been more willing to produce both clothing that is akin to fashion and one-of-a-kind wearable artworks intended for a gallery or museum audience, or to conceive of their fashion-oriented collections as wearable art. And as those lines blur, it has become increasingly difficult to tell the two apart.

A similar blurring has occurred between wearable art and fine art; the former has sacrificed wearability in the interest of artistic content while managing to remain identifiable as wearable art, while the popular use of unwearable garments as subject and metaphor in art has expanded to accept the use of wearable pieces in the same context.

Now seems an excellent time for an appraisal of wearable art. Although some artists of the original generation are still working, many others have stopped, or moved on to other genres, and a number of important galleries have closed. Yet there is evidence of increasing museum interest, with quite a few early pieces beginning to find their way into permanent collections. In both art and fashion there is a renewed fascination in the period that saw the birth of wearable art. There is also a new generation of artists not bound by the cultural framework of the 1970s, who seem likely to remake the genre in a new image. The boundaries separating artwear from fashion and art have softened, allowing artists to take a far more inclusive approach to all three disciplines. Moreover, they have new tools and new materials at their disposal, which, fused with traditional processes and materials, allow them to produce exciting new textiles to satisfy the public's appetite and their own for beautiful, tactile, handmade garments.

1·9 opposite

JUDITH CONTENT American (b. 1957)
Sweltering Sky, 1992
Thai silk; shibori-dyed and discharged, pieced, quilted, and appliquéd

This evocative landscape is in a kimono format but it is not proportioned for wearing.

Putting Artwear in Context

Jane Morris in Artistic Dress, 1865

John R. Parsons's photograph of Jane Morris, wife of William Morris, shows her in an early version of artistic dress. The dress, which hangs loose from the shoulders, suggests the fashionable line of the mid-1860s, but Morris appears to be wearing it without the conventional shaping undergarments of the period—a corset and a bell-shaped crinoline petticoat—beneath.

What Is Artwear?

Artwear is first and foremost an art of materials and processes whose creators are passionate about making art with textiles. Many of them have formal training in conventional fine and decorative arts and they have usually approached their work as artists, not as fashion designers. The art world, however, has accorded artwear halfhearted acceptance at best. The art press largely ignores it, as do virtually all galleries selling fine art. Relatively few American art museums collect it, and the majority of the wearable art exhibitions that have been mounted in museums since the 1970s have been organized by history, craft, or academic museums. Wearable art has been most closely identified with, and most freely accepted by, the studio craft world, where it is frequently featured in magazines such as *American Craft, Ornament, Surface Design Journal*, and *Fiberarts*, and with galleries and shows selling contemporary crafts. But even there, the craft hierarchy seems to put artwear at the bottom of the heap. A number of galleries that actively promote fiber art, for instance, do not show wearable art. I believe that this reflects the Western view that art should be purely contemplative and not functional, which leads us to place a higher value on the purely aesthetic than the object made for use. In addition, artwear's direct connection with the body suggests to some in the art and craft worlds an uncomfortably close link to fashion. In fact, artwear can be said to exist at the intersection between art, craft, and fashion. It is of all three, but is owned wholly by none of them.

Paving the Way

The art-versus-craft debate was ignited nearly a century and a half ago by the Arts and Crafts movement, and the impulses behind the wearable art of the 1970s and later can be traced back to this and all the related movements and schools—Art Nouveau, the Jugendstil, the Vienna Secession, the Bauhaus—that accompanied or followed it. All of them sought nothing less —or more—than to unite the roles of artist and craftsman. This drive to reorder the hierarchy of art and craft was very much in tune with Japanese custom, which traditionally does not distinguish between the two. The opening of Japan to the West in the 1850s began a flow of information and Japanese goods to Europe and the United States that sparked an intense wave of Japonisme, particularly after the Meiji empire was established in 1868. Japanese art was profoundly influential on Western decorative arts during the last quarter of the nineteenth century, and Japan's perceived adherence to pre-industrial ideals of fine craftsmanship—with its respect for materials, its reverence for nature, and the dignity of its craftspeople—was tremendously attractive to advocates of the Arts and Crafts and related movements.[1]

The Arts and Crafts movement had a social and political as well as an aesthetic agenda; it developed in Britain largely as a response to the Industrial Revolution and its widespread effects on society, especially the goods that society produced and consumed. The adherents of the movement were heavily influenced by philosopher and critic John Ruskin, who felt that the very health of society was threatened by the

DESIGNER UNKNOWN American
Aesthetic Evening Dress, ca. 1895–1900
Eggplant wool challis and pink and blue shot
silk taffeta

This American dress follows the classical ideal
of reform style, which featured a high Neo-
Classical waistline and puffed sleeves, often
with smocked or embroidered detail.

nature of industry, which separated the designer from the maker and elevated the manager far above the laborer. The cure was to be art, particularly decorative art, which would be produced in the traditional, handcrafted, pre-industrial way that upheld the joy and dignity of hand labor. Seizing on the increasing importance accorded to the decorative arts during the 1850s, the proponents of the Arts and Crafts movement essentially fired the opening volley in the endless battle to elevate the prestige of functional decorative arts to equal that of the functionless fine arts.

The lynchpin of the Arts and Crafts movement in Britain was the Victorian polymath William Morris. The prototype of the successful artist/designer/craftsman, he was the proprietor of the decorative arts firm Morris & Co., one of the most successful of its day. Morris & Co. employed other notable artists such as Dante Gabriel Rossetti and Edward Burne-Jones (both early partners in the firm) to design, and sometimes to execute, goods that ran the gamut of the decorative arts—virtually every kind of item one would need for the home *except* for clothing—all designed to facilitate the creation of an artistically unified environment.

What made Morris both so good and so influential as a designer was his passion for making things. He designed nothing that he did not know how to make, and often taught himself the necessary skills. His art and design work was the result of his explorations of just what his materials would and would not do. Perhaps ironically, he produced little of Morris & Co.'s output, leaving execution to a band of skilled employees or sometimes to outside firms. Nonetheless, his passion for handwork not only distinguished him as a designer, it was the precedent for virtually all the revival movements that followed his.

As Linda Parry has pointed out, Morris was deeply interested in textiles as a way of creating figurative art on a grand scale and beautiful home environments,[2] but not, I believe, for clothing. Indeed, most of those involved in the Arts and Crafts movement designed and created everything to provide a total artistic environment for the home, but rarely, if ever, essayed garments to decorate the body. The movement was, however, closely allied with nineteenth-century dress reform and artistic dress. Like the

proponents of the Arts and Crafts movement, the dress reformers were motivated by political and social aims as well as aesthetics. Women's fashionable clothing was seen as cumbersome and confining and symbolic of all that prevented women from achieving a more equal status with men. Many of the women who advocated dress reform in the 1870s and 80s were active in promoting women's suffrage, property rights, and higher education, and their views were decidedly anti-fashion. The most radical of the dress reformers recommended some sort of trouserlike garment for women, but most were content with clothes inspired by historical and Oriental models that had loose, unconstructed lines and that could be worn without corsets (1.11). This kind of dress was dubbed *Pre-Raphaelite* in the 1870s by Mary Haweis, a leading advocate, thus firmly associating it with the artistic circle from which Morris had sprung. The terms *aesthetic* and *artistic* dress, also used at the time, linked the reformers with the Aesthetic movement which, like the Arts and Crafts movement with which it overlapped, was also rooted in architecture and the decorative arts. The Aesthetic movement championed the idea that people's lives would be beautified if they surrounded themselves with beautiful objects, but Aesthetes departed from Ruskin's concept that art was to be the savior of industrialized society by prizing art simply for its sheer beauty, and not for any moral or functional role that it might play in society— "art for art's sake." Many artists associated with the Arts and Crafts movement, including Rossetti, Burne-Jones, E. W. Godwin, and Charles Rennie Mackintosh, were also Aesthetes, and it seems likely that their wives and daughters shared their views. Indeed, photographs and drawings of the families of the Pre-Raphaelite and Aesthetic movement artists are among the earliest representations we have of women wearing aesthetic dress (1.10).

Artistic dress, as a symbol that the wearer either moved in artistic circles or had the taste to appreciate them, became quite popular among certain sections of the upper and middle classes. By 1884, when its dress department opened, any lady desirous of wearing artistic dress could acquire it from Liberty's, the great London emporium for the artistically inclined. Liberty's employed the architect and Aesthete E. W.

Godwin as the first head of its dress department. The firm's success was founded on the importation of goods, including costume, from the East—kimonos, antique Japanese and Chinese embroidered coats, Turkish veils and shoes—but it did not produce its own clothes until ten years later, when Godwin decided to challenge the hegemony of high fashion through artistic dresses designed and sold by the department, even going so far as to open a branch in Paris. In contrast to the Arts and Crafts taste, which was firmly grounded on Gothic prototypes, artistic dress Liberty-style, though frequently in the unusual, muted colors favored by Morris and Burne-Jones, was characterized by a combination of Oriental and historical elements, in which the Middle Ages, the eighteenth century, the Near and Far East, and Ancient Greece can all be traced. Their nod to the Arts and Crafts philosophy was the hand-embroidery with which many were decorated (1.12).

In the United States as in Britain, artistic clothing was promoted by dress reformers for political and health reasons as well as aesthetic ones. The American Arts and Crafts and Aesthetic movements catered more to middle-class tastes than did their English predecessors, and were more commercial in their orientation. The prototypical American Arts and Crafts dress was one made of handwoven cloth (or cloth that looked handwoven) decorated with simple, pretty hand-embroidery, an important signifier. It generally followed the current line of fashion, deviating primarily in its surface decoration. Small accessories like handbags were also sold as embroidery kits for women to work at home.

The Arts and Crafts movement inspired a number of other artists, both those affiliated with other schools and movements and those working alone, to create artistic dress. The Omega Workshop, for example, a Post-Impressionist British artists' design collective founded in 1913 that included the painters Roger Fry, Vanessa Bell, and Duncan Grant, produced hand-painted clothing for men as well as women, though its output was small and its contemporary audience limited. The British reformers also influenced artists in other European countries, such as Henry van de Velde, a Belgian architect associated both with Art Nouveau and the Jugendstil, who was one of

the most active promoters of reform dress in Germany. Van de Velde designed and also lectured and wrote about artistic dress (1.13). Since the female realm at that time was still unquestionably domestic, it is probably not surprising that van de Velde explicitly identified women's dress as an important component of interior design and architecture.[3] Van de Velde was one of several artists designing reform dress on a relatively small scale in Germany at the time (many of whom used silks from Liberty's), but for dress production on a large scale, one must look to workshops like the Wiener Werkstätte.

The Wiener Werkstätte was founded in Vienna in 1903 by Secessionist Josef Hoffmann. Both the Secession and the Wiener Werkstätte lacked the social agenda that marked the Arts and Crafts movement; Wiener Werkstätte artist Vally Wieselthier articulated their goal as the desire to promote the idea that, in a well-ordered world, craft would not follow upon art, but rather art would grow from craftsmanship.[4] Artists were encouraged to work in several disciplines and expected to learn how to realize their own designs in virtually all media, although there were certainly instances where an artist merely supervised the making of his or her designs by other workers. The Wiener Werkstätte had both a textile and a fashion department, and while they were not created to operate in tandem, the fashion department was certainly encouraged to use the workshop's textiles, which were designed by a group of artists that included Hoffmann, Wieselthier, Dagobert Peche, and Maria Likarz. Gustav Klimt, though associated with the Wiener Werkstätte and thought to be interested in reform dress, is not recorded as having designed either textiles or fashions for it (1.15). Many of the artists who did design textiles for the Wiener Werkstätte—mainly women—also turned their hands to clothing; a number of their early efforts were loose-fitting reform-style dresses, and even after their work moved into mainstream fashion, consciousness of a reformist goal often seems evident. That may be why there are a number of Wiener Werkstätte at-home and lounging models featuring trousers, the adoption and acceptance of bifurcated garments for women being a major goal of the nineteenth-century dress reformers. Like Liberty's, the Wiener Werkstätte fashion department seems to have been quite successful

in creating clothing that was distinctive enough to appeal to the artistically inclined while remaining safely within fashion's general orbit (1.16). Again as at Liberty's, the fashion department at the Wiener Werkstätte was headed by an architect, Eduard Wimmer-Wisgrill, who had studied under Koloman Moser. Moser was particularly interested in reform dress, producing an entire reform collection in 1900 and subsequently making several dresses for the women in his family (1.14). Although he left the Wiener Werkstätte before the opening of the textile and dress departments, his influence was undoubtedly felt through Wimmer-Wisgrill.[5]

Artistic dress took a strongly Classical form in Venice in the work of Spanish-born Mariano Fortuny. Fortuny's clothes were initially considered extreme, but they eventually became the most successful and widely disseminated artist-designed clothing of the twentieth century. Fortuny, who trained as a painter, was influenced by a family collection of historic textiles, the art of the Aesthetic movement, and dress reformers. He began to experiment with textile printing around 1906 and in 1907 created the Delphos robe, named for the statue of the charioteer at Delphi and designed after the finely pleated and draped linen garments depicted on other ancient sculptures and in paintings. The Delphos, made of pleated and undulated custom-dyed silk, was Fortuny's ideal of proper, beautiful, and natural dress for women, and in the decades that followed he introduced only minor variations to his original design.[6] Fortuny also took a variety of ethnic garments as his models for the printed velvet and gauze coats and tunics he designed to be worn over Delphos dresses, including the kimono, djellabah, and burnous (1.17). Initially at least, he regarded the Delphos not as art but as an invention, even going so far as to patent his design.[7] Fortuny was no dressmaker, relying first on his wife and later on seamstresses to make the clothes, but he was a tremendously gifted dyer—as attested by the depth of color he achieved in both the Delphoses and the silk, gauze, and velvet tunics and coats. Fortuny's work prefigures a number of aspects of artwear, notably its concentration on technique and materials and its use of ethnic garments.

Changes in women's fashion, from the curvaceous and constricting styles popular prior

1·12 opposite

LIBERTY & CO. ARTISTIC AND HISTORIC COSTUME STUDIO British
Day Dress, ca. 1903
Raw silk pongee; smocked and embroidered with silk

Soft colors, smocking, and embroidery were three hallmarks of Liberty's artistic dresses.

1·13 above

Architect Henry van de Velde, who designed this lavishly embroidered velvet artistic dress, thought women's dress should emphasize the beauty of its materials.

to World War I to the clean, straight Modernist lines of the interwar period, helped pave the way for the acceptance not only of Fortuny's revealing Grecian dresses but also for the work of Sonia Delaunay, a Paris-based avant-garde painter and pioneer of Modernism, who completely integrated her work in both the fine and decorative arts. She believed that there was no difference between her paintings and her textiles, and indeed the similarity of the two bears her out. Delaunay was a brilliant colorist who evolved a vocabulary of geometric shapes that juxtaposed bright and neutral colors; when deployed on textiles and in clothing they expressed her sense of the shape of the body and the rhythms and emotions of life. She designed textiles both for industry and for her own fabric-printing workshop, and ran a very successful couture business in Paris during the 1920s and early 30s, producing clothes made from her own printed textiles and embroideries. Delaunay was unusual in conceiving the garment to be made from each textile as she designed it; initially she had the garment cutting lines printed on the textiles so that she could control exactly where each motif fell on the body.[8]

Unlike the dress reformers who preceded her, Delaunay was not anti-fashion; nor did she seek to change fashion to make it more "artistic." Her art was fully integrated in the design of the textiles and the cut of the garment. This was possible precisely because the prevailing silhouette in the 1920s was in tune with her aesthetic. When it evolved into the figure-hugging and flowing lines popular in the 1930s, she abandoned fashion design.

Delaunay's work with textiles and fashion in Paris coincided with the operations of the Bauhaus in Germany. The Bauhaus, which was founded by architect Walter Gropius in 1919 and was closed by the Nazis in 1933, is an important precursor to the studio fiber art movement that developed in the United States after World War II. Its connection to artwear is less direct, but its philosophy permeated the world of American art textiles, one of the frameworks within which wearable art exists. Like all the other Arts and Crafts–inspired schools, the Bauhaus was modeled on theories of the unity of art and craftsmanship; unusually, it subsequently embraced the marriage of art and technology. Its masters and students had

KOLOMAN MOSER Austrian (1868–1918)
Reform Dress, ca. 1905

This figure-concealing dress falls from a narrow yoke at the bust and can be worn without a corset. It was designed by Moser for his wife.

1·15 below left

Reform Dress Worn by Emilie Flöge, ca. 1907

Viennese fashion designer Flöge was a friend of artist Gustav Klimt and an early Wiener Werkstätte client; scholars disagree about whether or not Klimt was involved in the design of the reform dresses, such as this one, that Flöge both sold and wore.

1·16 opposite

FASHION STUDIO OF THE WIENER WERKSTÄTTE Austrian (1910–31)
Woman's Afternoon Dress, ca. 1917
Silk chiffon, net, and embroidery

The Wiener Werkstätte, which presented its first fashion collection in 1911, strove and largely succeeded in melding the demands of high fashion with reform ideals.

MARIANO FORTUNY Spanish, working in
Italy (1874–1949)
Delphos and Coat, 1930s
Dyed pleated silk satin and stencil-printed
dyed silk velvet

Fortuny gave his textiles their characteristically
complex, rich colors through repeated
dyeing. The motifs on the coat, which is simply
constructed of four loom-widths of velvet
joined at the sides and center back, were
inspired by Cretan art.

had formal training in the fine arts and came to the Bauhaus to teach or to learn about functional objects; however, unlike the Wiener Werkstätte, the Bauhaus had no interest in producing clothing. It did have an active and highly respected textile department—indeed, it has been argued that the textile department was the most successful of all the Bauhaus workshops[9]—but it was focused first on creating art textiles and later on creating handwoven prototypes for industry. In its embrace of industry and the machine age, the Bauhaus encouraged experimentation with new media and techniques; it moved away from the nostalgia that fueled Morris and many other reformers, and looked firmly forward.

It is possible that the lack of interest in clothing stemmed from the Bauhaus's focus on weaving (the Wiener Werkstätte, for instance, mainly produced printed textiles, which can be made by hand faster than woven ones). It is also possible that the changes between the ornate women's fashion of 1903, when the Wiener Werkstätte was founded, and the straight, body-skimming, lightweight clothes of the 1920s, when the Bauhaus was in its heyday, made fashion much less of a challenge to the reformist spirit.

One aspect of the Bauhaus that did reverberate, both for later fiber artists and for those making wearable art, was its conviction that textiles were women's work. Sigrid Weltge, in her study of the Bauhaus weaving workshop, relates that most of the women who applied to study at the Bauhaus—many of them with extensive prior training in the fine arts—were funneled to the textile workshop whether or not they had interest in and aptitude for weaving because, despite the official rhetoric, the directors of the school were not prepared to admit women to most of the other workshops.[10] That this was a disappointment to many women who hoped to study in other areas is certain. Nonetheless, the combination of rigorous training in weaving techniques and art instruction from the likes of Gropius, Paul Klee, Josef Albers, and Wassily Kandinsky produced artists who were passionate about their medium, and who sought to expand its technical horizons as far as they could. When they scattered in the wake of the Nazi rise to power, they passed their expertise and enthusiasm on to a new generation of students, many of them in the United States.

Feminism and the Fashion Trap

Many of the salient characteristics of these movements are present in wearable art: the value attached to textiles made by hand, the endless experimentation to see exactly how far a medium can be developed, the passion of the artists for their chosen media, the application of fine arts techniques, and the attempted distancing from fashion. And just as nineteenth-century dress reformers were allied with the nascent fight for women's rights, certain characteristics of artwear can perhaps best be understood in the context of the feminism of the 1960s and 70s, which sought equal rights, opportunities, and financial rewards for women within the male realm, and encouraged men to accept an equal share in the responsibilities and behaviors thought of as traditionally female. Art in the Western world has been and largely remains a male bastion, with women constantly seeking to scale the fortress walls, and it is only to be expected that recognition by the art world would be a goal for many art-school-trained women seeking enfranchisement. Feminism emboldened artists who were drawn to fiber and clothing to make art with them and strive to recontextualize as serious art what in another era would be dismissed as "women's work." Like their nineteenth-century predecessors, many mid-twentieth-century feminists saw fashion as a trap for women, which should be rejected or modified. Many of those making wearable art plainly felt that fashion was also a trap for them, so they, too, chose to renounce it. I believe artwear's widespread adoption of ethnic garment formats, particularly the kimono, is due more to its desire to separate itself from fashion than to an interest in non-Western cultures. Certainly the kimono's canvaslike structure invites a painterly approach, and it must have seemed very familiar to those with training in the fine arts. Artists who were envisioning their wearables hanging on the wall as much as on the body may have been inspired by the Japanese practice of displaying kimonos right-side-out on stands, with their front flaps spread out to form a triptych or a continuation of the picture plane. This display format has been widely copied by American artists, who often design kimonos that use the front panels to complement or extend the imagery on the back (1.22, 1.23).

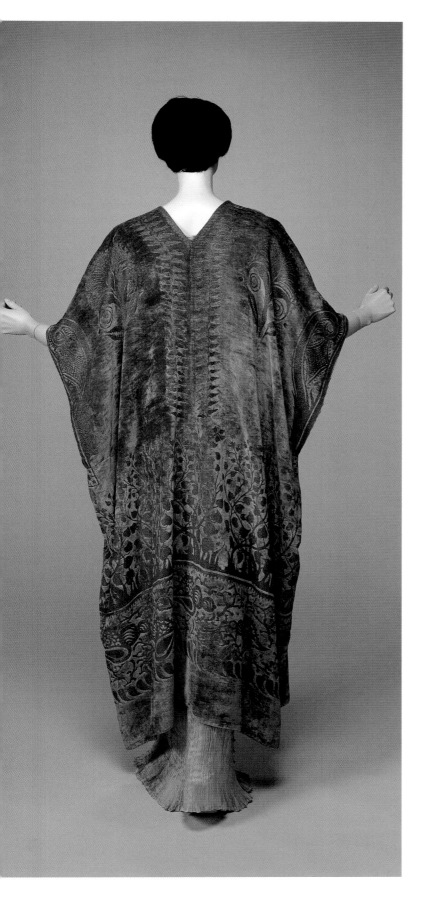

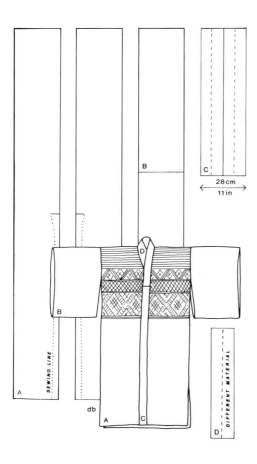

1·18 above

Diagram of a kimono from Dorothy Burnham's book, *Cut My Cote*. First published in 1973, the book was a popular resource for wearable art garments.

1·19 opposite

KANSAI YAMAMOTO Japanese (b.1944)
Dress, 1971
Wool and cotton ikat, leather, snakeskin

Yamamoto fuses a Western A-line dress with long kimono sleeves that serve as canvases for images modeled on specific Japanese *ukiyo-e* prints. Seattle artist Diana Aurigemma used a similar approach with Western images in a 1978 performance piece (5.5).

The kimono's simple cut and easy construction were a boon for artists not previously trained in fashion design and pattern-drafting and who wanted to maintain their distance from fashion by not gaining the knowledge. Kimonos became widely available both as models and as potential sources of textiles to be recycled into artwear from 1973 on, when Ruby Uehara, then in Honolulu, formed the Orizaba Company and began importing vintage kimonos to North America and Europe by the bale.[11] Moreover, the kimono's adoption into wearable art was positively reinforced by its concurrent use in painting by artists such as Miriam Schapiro, as a symbol of the new, liberated woman.[12] But most important, the kimono is an example of what art historian Anne Hollander has dubbed *nonfashion*: an ethnic (that is, non-Western) garment that represents tradition and established custom, and offers a distinctive and relatively unchanging form, beautiful color and pattern, and many levels of symbolic meaning.[13] This is diametrically opposed to the way Western fashion operates, so the kimono must have seemed an ideal choice for artists wanting to make a clear distinction between their work and fashion.

Paradoxically, the kimono—stripped of its traditional context and meaning—has also been popular in Western fashion since the third quarter of the nineteenth century,[14] periodically remade in the fashionable image of the moment. As it happens, it was made fashionable in the 1960s and early 70s by Western designers like Rudi Gernreich and the Japanese designers just entering Western fashion—Hanae Mori, Kansai and Yohji Yamamoto, Kenzo, Rei Kawakubo, and Issey Miyake (1.19). Their model, which became dominant in fashion in the 1980s when Japan was a formidable economic and cultural force in the West, often fused traditional, humble, or luxurious Japanese garments with Western fashionable dress (1.21). The kimono reappeared in fashion in the 1990s when Paris regained its fashion leadership (1.20). Since wearable art chose the kimono in part because it is non-fashion, there is tremendous irony in its continued popularity in fashion during the past thirty years.

The kimono was not, of course, the only traditional garment that artists chose, and in the 1970s two books were instrumental in providing them with a range of options. Dorothy Burnham's *Cut my Cote* (1.18), published in 1973, explained that the reasons behind the cut of traditional European and ethnic garments were rooted in the shape of the animal skins or the loom widths of the cloth from which they were first made. In addition to photographic examples of each style, the book provided simple diagram patterns of each shirt, shift, robe, coat, and kimono. Max Tilke's *Costume Patterns and Designs,* originally published in 1956 and reprinted in the early 1970s, offered color plates and occasional diagrams of hundreds of traditional garments from all over the world. Although, in general, artwear has slowly evolved in a more fashion-conscious direction, nonfashion garment forms have remained important and form a kind of signature of the genre.

What's in a Name?

The term *wearable art*, which I have chosen to use throughout this book interchangeably with *artwear* and *art to wear*, was first used around 1975, and it quickly caught on as a handy way to describe what was then often called *body art*.[15] It should be said, however, that many practitioners and dealers dislike the name. The important dealer Julie Schafler Dale of Julie: Artisans' Gallery in New York has said that she was never comfortable with *wearable art* and selected *Art to Wear* as the title of her seminal 1986 book because she felt the inverted phrase was more dignified.[16] For some, the dislike arises from their continuing struggle for recognition from the art world. Artist Jean Williams Cacicedo has pointed out that ceramics are not called *art to throw*, nor glass *art to blow*,[17] and that by extension, attaching the modifier *wearable* to the noun *art* implies that such garments would not otherwise be considered art. Others take exception to the broadening of its definition to include amateur work by the large and enthusiastic population who make wearable art as an avocation, and the wide variety of art-tinged fashion that the media dubs *wearable art*, particularly those designs that reproduce, either in facsimile or in modified form, the image of a work of art originally made in another medium. It is understandable that there would be concerns about the resulting confusion

surrounding the term in the public mind, but the fact that ideas of what constitutes wearable art have broadened and continue to change is, I think, positive. Though many have tried, no one has come up with a single alternative term that has been as widely accepted as *wearable art* and so it and the inverse *art to wear* have remained in active use.

Nowadays, the identification of a garment as *wearable art* rather than *fashion* may have as much to do with the artist's self-identification with the wearable art or contemporary fiber art community, or the size and capitalization of the concern that produced it (artwear tends to be made by artists working either alone or in a studio or cottage-industry set-up, with limited output and financial resources), as it does with the garment's form, aesthetic characteristics, or intended use. The narrow definition of *wearable art* has given way to a continuum that begins perhaps with garments that are technically but not actually wearable, and ends with luxurious, handmade ready-to-wear aimed at a fashion-aware clientele. The stops along the way include grand one-of-a-kind pieces with serious content that are intended to be displayed on the wall as well as on the body, limited-edition production, and costumes worn for performance.

1·20 opposite

The kimono reappears periodically in high fashion. In this 1999 fashion photograph by Patrick Demarchelier, a serene Madonna wears a kimono by Jean-Paul Gaultier and an obilike corset by Dolce & Gabbana.

1·21 above

REI KAWAKUBO FOR COMME DES GARÇONS Japanese (b.1942)
Woman's Coat, mid-1980s
Wool with cotton stitching

Kawakubo's coat suggests a worker's kimono with its folded-up sleeves and plain, dark fabric scored with lines of sashikolike stitching.

1·22 above

DEBORAH VALOMA American (b. 1955)
Moment in Thebes, 1987
Wool; pieced and appliquéd

The motifs on Valoma's bright pieced and appliquéd coats convey an impression of depth and movement. The coat's title alludes to her interests in history, archaeology, and anthropology, while her deft handling of its form reflects her training at Fashion Institute of Technology.

1·23 opposite

SHARRON HEDGES American (b. 1948)
Desert Ikat, 1989
Loom-knitted wool and other fibers

Knitted rather than woven as ikats traditionally are, this coat nonetheless has an ikat's characteristically soft-edged imagery.

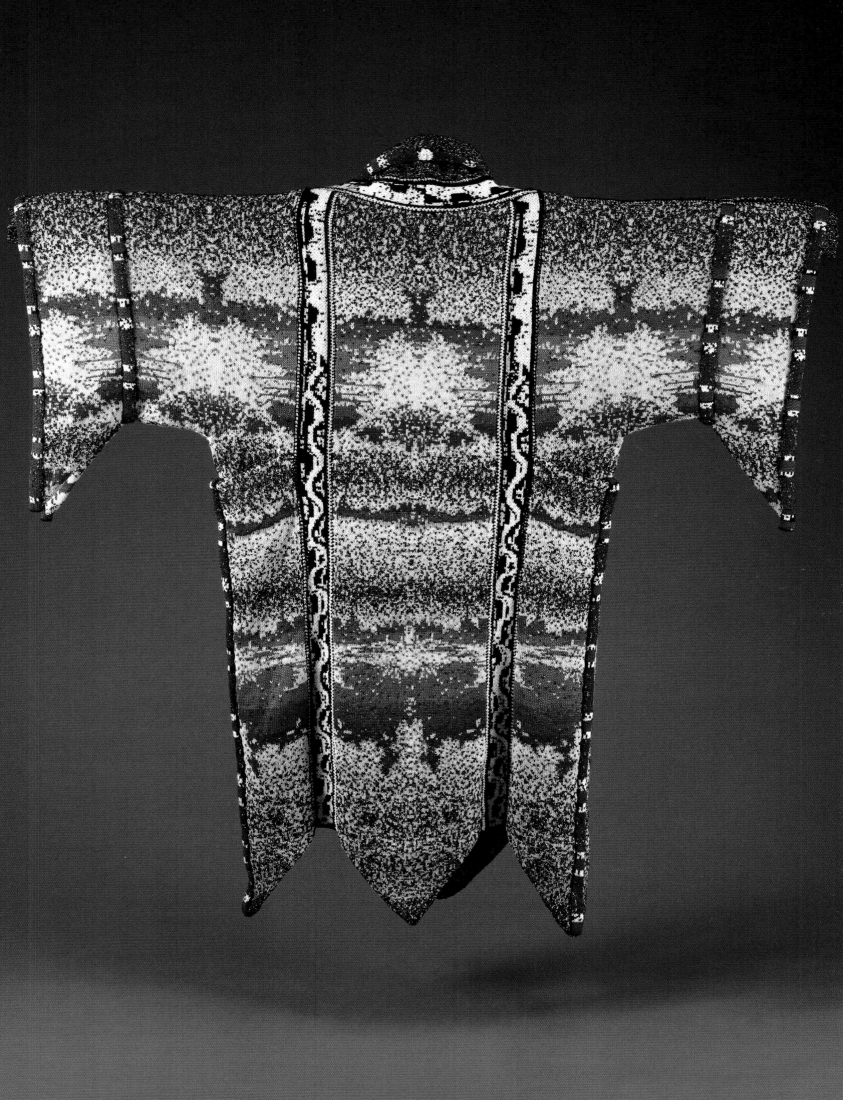

2   Artwear in the U.S.A.

2·1 below

Janis Joplin posed for *Rolling Stone* photographer Baron Wolman in her Haight-Ashbury home in 1967 wearing a pantsuit made for her by Linda Gravenites from a recycled lace tablecloth.

2·2 opposite

JULIA HILL working in U.S.
(b. Germany, 1947)
American Velvet, 1988
Painted silk velvet

Hill's coat was one of the dozen pieces of wearable art that toured Europe with *Craft Today: USA*, an exhibition organized by the American Craft Museum.

Artwear developed simultaneously in New York and the San Francisco Bay Area in the late 1960s and early 70s. Although very much an anti-fashion movement, it grew from West Coast street style. At the beginning of the 1960s, France still dominated American fashion, even if its hold on fashion trends was already being weakened by youthful and working-class street style. The first baby boomers came of age in the early to mid-1960s and firmly rejected their parents' values and modes of living, and with it their fashions. Instead, they wore clothes that were young, energetic, idealistic, futuristic, romantic, even hopeful. Mod fashion, from designers like Mary Quant, Ossie Clark, and Barbara Hulanicki (Biba), developed in London and swiftly spread across the Atlantic. It was short, streamlined, and youthful; featured large-scale floral or geometric imagery; and often used new and unusual materials. New York's version was most readily to be had at the seminal boutique Paraphernalia, whose stable of designers included Betsey Johnson along with the major London names; Los Angeles had Rudi Gernreich (2.6). Mod styles were a strong influence on hippie fashion, which developed on the West Coast and swiftly spread east with the help of musicians like Janis Joplin, Jefferson Airplane, and Tina Turner, many of whom were photographed both on and off the stage wearing beautiful handmade clothes by San Francisco designers Linda Gravenites and Jeanne Rose (2.1).

Both Mod and hippie fashion appealed to a community of young people who loved to dress up and decorate themselves. Hippie styles were more romantic, psychedelic, and ornate than Mod, but the two shared the idea that people should express—explicitly, honestly, and through their clothing—their real inner selves, their thoughts, aspirations, beliefs, or even just aspects of their daily lives.[1] Connected to this was the high value placed on handmade things, which were seen as having a soul and an integrity that industrially produced goods lacked—an idea that was a catalyst for wearable art (2.3, 2.4).[2] The hippie look featured hand embellishment—embroidery, painting, tie-dyeing—on new or well-worn and vintage clothing found in thrift shops, which ideally was customized by its wearers or their friends and family (2.8), but it could also be bought commercially. Ethnic textiles and garments were also popular and increasingly available (2.5), reflecting both the Peace Corps service and extensive traveling done by many young Americans in Africa, Asia, and Latin America, and Americans' general rising interest in and knowledge of non-Western cultures (2.12).

One measure of how deeply this particular form of folk art had permeated the culture both in America and abroad was the Levi Strauss Denim Contest, staged in 1974. The nationally advertised contest invited people from across the United States to submit pictures of their hand-decorated denims for evaluation by a panel of distinguished judges that included photographer Imogen Cunningham and designer Rudi Gernreich (2.7). The judges waded through 10,000 slides (representing about 2,000 entries) of dyed, pieced, patched, painted, appliquéd, embroidered, beaded, studded, quilted,

2·3 top

K. LEE MANUEL American (1936–2003)
Evening Dress (center), ca. 1968; *Tunics*,
ca. 1965
Painted cotton

These early wearable artworks demonstrate
the simple cut and intricate, obviously hand-
decorated surfaces that would come to
characterize the genre in the following decade.

crocheted, macraméd, and hooked jeans and
jackets, and selected fifty winners (2.10), whose
handiwork was published in a catalogue by
former *Rolling Stone* chief photographer Baron
Wolman. The traveling exhibition of these
works appeared at a half-dozen museums
across the country, including the Museum of
Contemporary Crafts in New York, the Walker
Art Center in Minneapolis, and the de Young
Museum in San Francisco. The contest was
so successful that Levi's staged smaller versions
in several European countries the following
year (2.9).

1970s: Artwear Comes of Age

Hippie style was actually on its way out by the
time of the Levi's contest, but wearable art in
both the Bay Area and in New York was already
established and moving toward an identity
distinct from fashion. In New York, the
movement coalesced around a small group
of undergraduate art students at Pratt Institute
of Art. Jean Williams Cacicedo learned to
crochet during the summer of 1968 and taught

it to her roommates, Janet Lipkin and Marika
Contompasis. Soon, all were obsessed by crochet
and began to incorporate it into their artwork.
Pratt had no fiber art program at that time and
the students from the art school did not mix
with the fashion department, so the three were
able to explore freely, there being no one to
teach them formally. As Lipkin later commented,
"we went nuts" (2.14).[3] Fortunately, Pratt was
remarkably accepting of artwork in unusual
media from its students, and the crochet was
no exception.[4] Lipkin was particularly
enamored; crochet was portable so she could
make art literally wherever she was. A further
attraction was that it allowed her simultaneously
to acknowledge the heritage of needlework in
her family and to set herself apart from her
fellow painters at Pratt, because no one else
sewed or crocheted.[5] Lipkin's early work was
sculpture rather than garments, but soon all
three women, along with their Pratt colleagues
Sharron Hedges and Dina Knapp (2.11), were
crocheting clothes and teaching their techniques
to others, and they helped to create a community
of people in New York making wearable art.

2·4 opposite below

Mary Ann Schildknecht models a shirt she made from a bedsheet that she tore into pieces and covered with embroidery. Schildknecht's tour-de-force is among the most accomplished pieces of embroidered artwear known.

2·5 above left

YVONNE PORCELLA American (b. 1936)
Short Tunic, ca. 1971
Cotton, mirror cloth, found objects

This tunic's mix of textiles, which includes Indian mirror cloth and molas made by the Kuna people of Panama's San Blas Islands, reflects contemporary interest in non-Western cultures.

2·6 above right

RUDI GERNREICH Austrian, working in U.S. (1922–1985)
Kimono Dress, 1968
Printed silk, metallic brocade, vinyl

Gernreich interprets the kimono as a Western mini-dress made of a Japonesque print, dominated by a prominent checked obilike sash.

CALL FOR
ENTRIE

DENIM CLOTHING
AS ART

"they got tired of blue" ..... Imogen

clancy©

2·7 opposite

JUDITH CLANCY American (1933–1990)
They Got Tired of Blue, 1974
Ink and colored pencil on paper

Clancy's montage of the Levi's contest judging portrays judges, models, and Bill Shire's first-prize-winning jacket. The drawing's title was a judge's comment about a garment so laden with embroidery that no denim was visible.

2·8 above left

In her book *Native Funk and Flash* (1974), Alexandra Jacopetti described how she gradually embroidered her husband Roland's worn Levi's shirt with motifs reflecting their lives and community. The embroidery, which symbolized her love and caring, imbued the decorated shirt with talismanic power.

2·9 above right **2·10** left

Peggy Moulton's embroidered *Tree of Life* and Doug Miles's painted Levi's were among the contest's twelve fourth-place winners. These are their contest entry photos.

2·11 below

SHARRON HEDGES American (b. 1948)
Vest, 1970
Crocheted wool

An example of the crochet being produced by
the young New York artists for themselves and
their friends to wear, and for sale.

2·12 right

DEL PITT FELDMAN American
Dress, ca. 1971
Crocheted rayon ribbon, cordé and twist
cordé, mirrors, beads

Feldman operated Studio Del, the yarn store
where many of the New York crocheters
congregated. The stylized Albino Indian figure
on the front panel of this dress was inspired
by a trip she took to Guatemala.

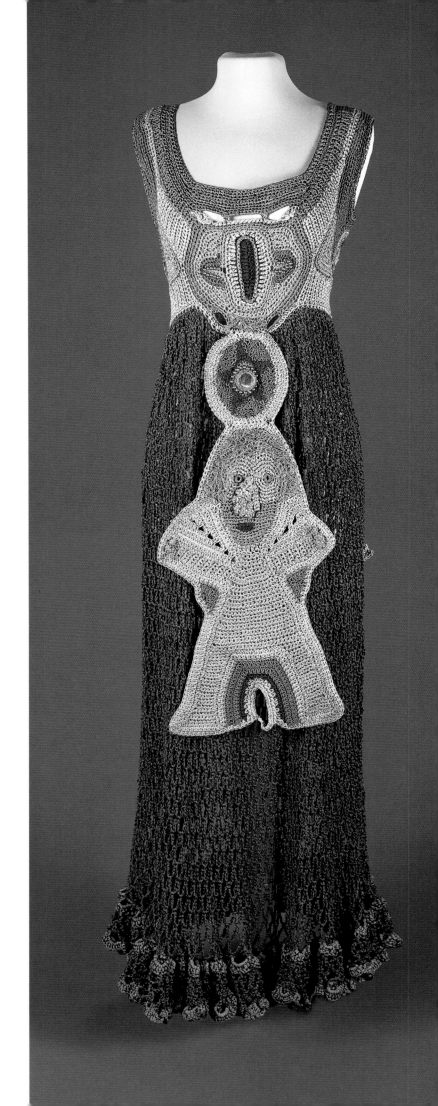

2·13 above

KAISIK WONG American (1950–1990)
Merle Bulatao in Chinatown, ca. 1978
Gelatin silver print

Bulatao wears a knee-length Guatemalan cotton jumpsuit from one of Wong's rare ready-to-wear collections. Wong, a gifted photographer, generally photographed his work outdoors on a favorite model as the culmination of his design process.

2·14 right

JANET LIPKIN American (b. 1948)
Ensemble, *African Mask*, 1970
Hand-spun and -dyed crocheted wool, leather, wood

Lipkin's riotously crocheted winter coat, hood, and mittens envelop and transform the wearer into a kinetic African sculpture.

2·15 below

FRED E. KLING American (b. 1944)
Dragon Skirt, ca. 1974
Painted cotton

Front and back views of Kling's maxi skirt demonstrate his fondness for wrapping large-scale imagery around the body.

2·16 opposite

FRED E. KLING American (b. 1944)
Wedding Dress, 1972
Painted cotton

Kling's dresses and skirts were made in collaboration with his wife Candace, who did the cutting and sewing, and were sold through several of the Bay Area boutiques.

The artwear that was simultaneously emerging in the Bay Area was different from the work coming out of New York. Its artists, who included Nancy Chappell, Marian Clayden, Fred and Candace Kling, K. Lee Manuel, and Kaisik Wong, among many others, were creating handmade clothes with paint, dye, and collage. Wong, a collagist with an abiding interest in ethnic textiles, was essentially working as an industry-trained couturier with his own small ready-to-wear business (2.13). Clayden, not yet herself making clothing, was dyeing fabric for the touring companies of the musical *Hair* (a production on which Manuel also worked) and collaborating with New Yorker Ben Compton on art garments. Manuel and the Klings were making vibrantly hand-painted clothes to trade and to sell locally (2.15, 2.16). Like the Pratt students, most were formally trained fine artists who happened to discover in themselves an utter fascination with textiles. Unusually, Wong and Candace Kling also had training in pattern-making.

It is impossible to overestimate how exciting a place the Bay Area was for textile aficionados in the late 1960s and 70s. A disproportionately large number of textile artists were living, working, and teaching there, and, according with the spirit of the times, they willingly and openly shared their ideas and artwork with each other without fear of its being diluted or copied.[6] There were important studio textile programs at the University of California campuses at Berkeley and Davis, at California College of Arts and Crafts, and at a number of independent organizations, such as the Yarn Depot, Pacific Basin School of Textile Arts, and Fiberworks Center for the Textile Arts, where the textile-minded could meet, learn, share ideas, and exhibit their work. The independent programs were particularly key for artists with fine arts but nontextile backgrounds, and Fiberworks, which opened in 1973, was probably the most significant of these organizations for the artwear community. It offered classes in a wide variety of textile techniques plus an exhibition venue

2·17 below

Kaisik Wong's jacket, wrap pant-skirt, and hat, shown here in a 1972 *Harper's Bazaar* photo alongside a kimono by Japanese fashion designer Hanae Mori, was produced as ready-to-wear under the Muuntux label, and could be purchased at Henri Bendel in New York. Wong, who envisioned many of his garments as unisex, is the model.

2·18 opposite

ANA LISA HEDSTROM American (b. 1943)
Waves, 1988
Shibori-dyed silk

In the *arashi* shibori technique, the fabric is compressed, often into pleats that resist the dye. Here the ironed-out pleating shows as the thin horizontal stripes of the coat's wave pattern.

for many of the local artists who were making one-of-a-kind pieces. Fiberworks held many exhibitions of wearable art during its fifteen-year life; the first, organized in 1974, was *Art Couture*, which was a runway-style fashion show rather than an installation. Later that same year, the art department at the Oakland Museum mounted *Bodywear*, the first major West Coast museum exhibition devoted to the broad range of artwear.

Fiberworks was also responsible for a watershed event in the history of wearable art: a class in shibori-dyeing techniques taught by Yoshiko Wada and Donna Larsen in 1975. Shibori is a general Japanese term encompassing a variety of resist-dyeing techniques that involve shaping cloth by folding, crumpling, stitching, plaiting, plucking and twisting, binding, or knotting it before dyeing. The kind of tie-dyeing found in hippie fashion is an extremely simple form of shibori.[7] At the time, Wada, who had trained as a textile artist in Kyoto and subsequently as a painter and printmaker at the University of Colorado, did not have much experience in this form of dyeing,[8] but she was knowledgeable enough to teach the class. Wada may be the single most important reason Japanese dyeing processes and terminology became so widespread in wearable art in America and elsewhere. Her seminal 1983 book, *Shibori: The Inventive Art of Japanese Resist Dyeing*, introduced readers to the history of shibori and its contemporary innovative uses in textile art in Japan and America, and offered easy-to-read shaping and binding diagrams for a variety of patterns. Hundreds of artists were introduced to these techniques through the book and her classes and workshops, and many have gone on to teach others, notably Ana Lisa Hedstrom. One of Wada's students at that first workshop, she herself became a master dyer and respected teacher of the process known as *arashi* shibori, in which the fabric to be dyed is wrapped around a cylinder (Hedstrom uses PVC pipe) and compressed into tight pleats that then resist the dye (2.18).

Hedstrom's influence is tied not only to her teaching and instructional videos but to her considerable body of very high quality work, which is widely shown. Wada and Hedstrom were also active, in collaboration with a group of other fiber artists, in forming a professional society dedicated to shibori.[9] Thanks in large part to their activities, a substantial network of

shibori-dyers has formed in the thirty years since that first Fiberworks class, and shibori has become one of the techniques most characteristic of artwear.

New York did not, perhaps, have as cohesive a fiber art community at this time but wearable art was also flourishing there and, significantly, it received museum attention early. Paul Smith, then director of the Museum of Contemporary Crafts (subsequently known as the American Craft Museum, and now the Museum of Arts and Design) was an early supporter and regularly included it in the museum's exhibitions. The first was *Body Covering* in 1968, which sought to explore both the functional and aesthetic aspects of clothing[10] in the form of an unusual mix of cutting-edge high fashion from designers like Rudi Gernreich and Paco Rabanne, performance costume, and handmade art clothing. *Body Covering* was followed by many other shows that focused on specific kinds of garments, including *Fur and Feathers* (1971), *Homage to the Bag* (1976), and *The Great American Foot* (1978).

Developing the Market

Few of the artists thought about selling their work at first. They made pieces for themselves, as gifts and to trade with others, for performance, and for exhibition. But a market quickly developed. Initially, wearable art was sold primarily through boutiques and small entrepreneurs or supporters who hosted trunk shows in their homes. There were quite a number of the former in the Bay Area, particularly in San Francisco and Berkeley: Family and Friends, Sew What, The Chair Store, White Duck Workshop, and By Hand. All either sold clothing exclusively or sold contemporary crafts that included artwear. Some also offered their own extremely well-made lines of clothing; The Chair Store and White Duck Workshop specialized in patchwork and appliqué, and Sew What in tie-dye (2.19). In New York, D. D. Dominicks and Studio Del were two of the retail options. Studio Del was primarily a yarn store, but it offered the crocheters from Pratt a place to teach their craft to others and offer their work for sale, and a community of interested artists developed around it. Large, high-fashion retailers on both coasts also took some interest; for example, in the early 1970s Kaisik Wong was selling his

ready-to-wear Muuntux line through both Henri Bendel in New York and I. Magnin & Co. in San Francisco (2.17).

Galleries followed quickly on the heels of boutiques and department stores. Many of the major American craft galleries opened their doors in the early to mid-1970s—The Hand and the Spirit in Scottsdale, Arizona; the Helen Drutt Gallery in Philadelphia; Mobilia in Cambridge, Massachusetts; Del Mano in Los Angeles; and Meyer, Breier, Weiss and Braunstein/Quay in San Francisco. These and a number of others gave artists places to show and sell their work in a gallery context in company with other studio crafts. Craft fairs, both major and minor, like the annual series run by the American Crafts Council and the Rhinebeck Fair in New York, provided additional opportunities within the studio craft market (2.20). And in 1973, the two seminal artwear galleries both opened: Obiko in San Francisco and Julie: Artisans' Gallery in New York.

Julie Schafler (now Julie Schafler Dale) opened Julie: Artisans' Gallery at 684 Madison Avenue in September 1973. Prior to that, the gallery was housed in her Manhattan apartment, where she showed by appointment and advertised primarily by word of mouth. Dale first became interested in wearable art around 1971, while pursuing graduate studies in art history at New York University and beginning to explore the contemporary art and craft scenes. Her longstanding interest in unusual and ethnic clothing was no doubt another factor. While doing some research at the Museum of Contemporary Crafts, Dale became excited by clothing she saw in slides from the *Fur and Feathers* and *Body Covering* exhibitions. Inspired, she collected artists' names and addresses from the museum and began to contact and visit them. She recalls their studios as oases filled with extraordinary things: "wonderful crocheted and tufted boots and painted, quilted jackets and feathered affairs."[11] Dale left those studios carrying bags full of exciting clothes, which formed the stock she sold from her apartment. When it became clear that she needed a commercial space, Dale chose Madison Avenue for its high visibility. As an upscale retail area full of galleries and boutiques, it must have seemed the ideal location to attract the kind of patron she hoped to interest in art to wear.

Obiko rose from the ashes of the San Francisco boutique Muuntux, opened in 1972 by Rita Chan and Kaisik Wong to sell Wong's clothing and Orientalia gathered by Chan. Wong's involvement with Muuntux[12] lasted only a few months and the boutique, renamed The

2·19 opposite

WHITE DUCK WORKSHOP
American (active 1960s–70s)
Maxi Dress, ca. 1970
Appliquéd cotton

2·20 above left

Ina Kozel's booth at the Rhinebeck (N.Y.) Crafts Fair in 1981.

2·21 above right

A window display at Obiko in San Francisco, designed and installed by Kaisik Wong.

2·22 below

LEA DITSON American (b. 1950)

Coat, mid-1980s

Silk; dyed and pieced

Ditson was one of the artists who started early with Sandra Sakata at Obiko, and whose career Sakata nurtured.

Great Eastern Trading Company, lasted only a few months after his departure. When it failed, its manager, Sandra Sakata, took charge of the remaining stock and began operating by appointment from her dining room. Late in 1973, at the urging of her roommates, the jewelry artists Alex and Lee, she opened Obiko at 3294 Sacramento Street in San Francisco. With the involvement once again of Kaisik Wong, who provided a large proportion of the store's initial stock and whose display skills gave its small windows a distinctive look, Obiko quickly became known as the place to go for unusual, one-of-a-kind, handmade clothing in the Bay Area (2.21). Obiko's slate of artists were primarily West Coast–based, whereas Dale's included a wider geographical range. A number of artists showed at both.

Long-term success for an artist usually includes gallery representation, exhibition in group and solo gallery and museum shows, coverage by the art press, sale of work to private collectors, and, finally, acquisition of work, either by purchase or donation, by a museum. It is to Julie Schafler Dale's credit that she realized that the existence of a gallery rather than a boutique was crucial in gaining an artist an art-world-style career, and so she created a gallery. Dale has been absolutely consistent in conceiving of her business as a gallery and her role as an art dealer whose job it is to nurture and encourage her artists to do their best work, and then to sell those pieces to the right collector. She has also carefully promoted her gallery and her artists through books, magazine articles, and advertising. Like any other art gallery, she mounts regular shows for her artists. Her approach is not unique; many of the other studio craft galleries operate in this way, but Dale has an extremely high profile, and she shows clothing and jewelry exclusively.

Sandra Sakata took a different approach at Obiko, which moved to the Union Square shopping district in 1978. Unlike Dale, she did not make a clear distinction between boutique and gallery. In many ways her small store felt more like a private home that happened to have display windows. One wall of the store was lined with deep closets packed full of clothes, each with a garment displayed hanging on the door; upstairs was a tiny boudoir for evening and special-occasion clothes.[13] Like Dale, Sakata nurtured her artists and developed deep relationships with a number of them, especially those whom she represented in Obiko's early days (2.22). She was extremely excited by the work of her artists,[14] and the careers of many of them relied on her support and her sales skills. Sakata's methods were fashion-oriented; she created ensembles for her clients, often combining pieces by several artists with some of the marvelous jewelry she also sold. Indeed, this ability was the key to her success. For many years Sakata's clientele was primarily West Coast–based, and her advertising was largely by word of mouth and through the regular fashion shows for which she was famous. But in 1982 she was approached by Bergdorf-Goodman's president Dawn Mello to open an Obiko shop within the department store. Sakata agreed; the Bergdorf's concession opened in November 1983.

1980s: The Move to Multiples

The wearable art Sakata sold at Bergdorf's was essentially distinctive, deluxe ready-to-wear; beautiful garments made from handmade textiles, which would stand out from ordinary ready-to-wear but which fell close enough to the general range of fashion to make wearers feel special but not as if they were in costume. Shortly after the boutique opened, *Women's Wear Daily* described Obiko's clothes as "unconstructed and loose, with a keen sense of texture blended with color (2.23),"[15] adding that the typical Bergdorf's Obiko customer was a couture wearer who bought her pieces as museum-quality items that could be worn for many years. Sakata selected each season's colors and gave her artists color samples and guidelines for length and shape. Although she did not otherwise seek to channel their creativity, she would not necessarily simply accept what they produced. Instead, she chose specifically what she wanted from what they offered her.[16] Both Dale and Sakata showed limited-edition pieces as well as one-of-a-kind work, and this enabled them to offer wearable art at a wider range of prices. Sakata, especially, needed the production work to keep up with the demand generated by two stores and pushed a number of her artists in that direction.

By the 1980s, artwear had well-established pathways of distribution and a solid client base nationally. Although some of its early

2.23 above

ANA LISA HEDSTROM American (b. 1943)
Crepe de Chine Coat, 1993
Silk; resist-dyed and pieced

Hedstrom's coat exemplifies the kind of
luxurious, unstructured, beautifully textured
and colored artwear that attracted women
who wished to feel artfully dressed.

practitioners had moved on to other fields,
a significant number of artists were making
a wide variety of art clothing using many
different techniques. The New York scene
remained vibrant, but by the end of the 1970s
a number of the early New York–based artists
had moved elsewhere: Dina Knapp, one of the
original Pratt artists, moved to Florida, and
three of her classmates—Lipkin, Cacicedo, and
Contompasis—landed in the Bay Area, where
Lipkin and Cacicedo remain. Museums all over
the country—even a few art museums[17]—were
mounting artwear exhibitions, with the most
significant and consistent attention paid by
the American Craft Museum as part of
its continuing coverage of developments

in contemporary fiber. It staged a pair of
exhibitions called *Art to Wear: New Handmade
Clothing*, the first in 1983 and the second the
following year, both accompanied by small,
nicely illustrated catalogues.[18] In 1986, wearable
art was included in *Craft Today: The Poetry
of the Physical*, a survey exhibition across all
craft media; its traveling version, *Craft Today
U.S.A.*, visited twelve European countries
between 1989 and 1992 (2.2). Also in the 1980s,
the fashion and the art media, though never
lavish with their coverage, began to pay the
genre some attention, and a lot of interest was
generated by Julie Schafler Dale in 1986 with the
publication of her lavishly illustrated book *Art
to Wear*, which highlighted the histories and

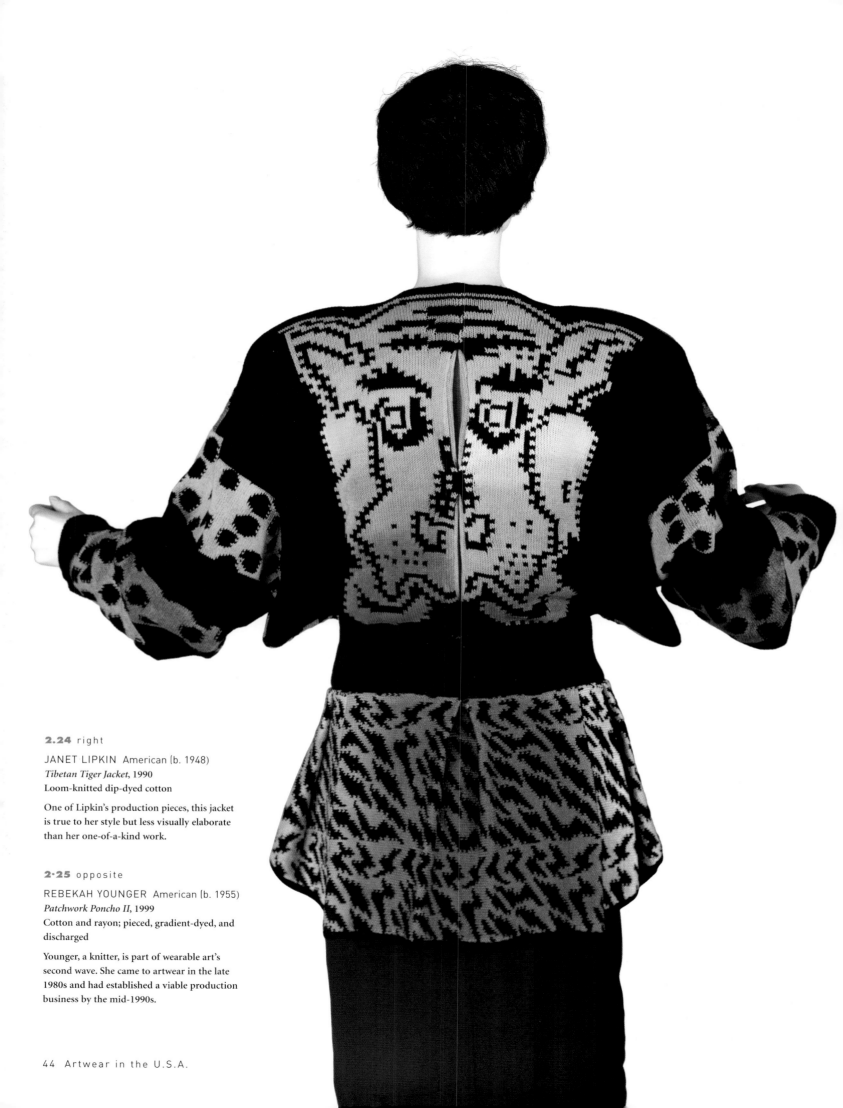

2.24 right

JANET LIPKIN American (b. 1948)
Tibetan Tiger Jacket, 1990
Loom-knitted dip-dyed cotton

One of Lipkin's production pieces, this jacket
is true to her style but less visually elaborate
than her one-of-a-kind work.

2.25 opposite

REBEKAH YOUNGER American (b. 1955)
Patchwork Poncho II, 1999
Cotton and rayon; pieced, gradient-dyed, and
discharged

Younger, a knitter, is part of wearable art's
second wave. She came to artwear in the late
1980s and had established a viable production
business by the mid-1990s.

work of sixty-one artists grouped by their signature processes.

The exuberance that characterized much of the 1970s work had waned by the end of the decade, replaced by sleeker cloth, greater sophistication, and an increased willingness to consider wearable art's wearability, particularly among those who were choosing to become involved in limited production. During the 1980s there was a noticeable shift in emphasis from one-of-a-kind to limited-edition production: a number of the artists who established themselves in the 1970s chose to start making limited-edition pieces (2.24). For many, the decision was purely economic; making important, one-of-a-kind pieces is very time-consuming and most artists could not earn a living from it. In the early days, many of the artists were living like the students they had only recently ceased to be, content to earn enough from their work to pay the rent and buy whatever materials they needed for the next piece. By the 1980s, maturity and the adult responsibilities of homes, spouses, and children meant that subsistence was no longer enough.

The 1980s also saw a second wave of artists who were too young to have been hippies in the 1960s but who nonetheless were excited about artwear (2.25). Some started off as had their predecessors, laboriously creating the textiles and from them major one-of-a-kind works, but many chose instead to create limited editions. For most, that essentially meant starting small fashion design businesses; acquiring staff, sales reps, and wholesale clients; doing less of the textile-making themselves; and moderating their artistic ideas and the style of their garments the better to conform to the fashion of the moment.

Production has been a thorny issue for wearable art. The difference between one-of-a-kind and limited production is analogous to the difference between haute couture and ready-to-wear, or the difference between a painting and a print. Both art and studio craft establishments have tended to be dismissive of multiples, regarding them as lesser than individual works, especially when the art is also functional and thereby uncomfortably close to the world of commerce. This attitude has carried over into artwear, where the tendency has been to attach higher value to one-of-a-kind than to limited-edition work. Certainly, unique works are usually more ambitious and may be more artistically expressive than edition work, but the fact that they are one-of-a-kind is not a surefire guarantee of quality. Many artists undoubtedly

find it more satisfying to create single art pieces than repeat themselves for multiples; but, on the other hand, less expensive limited-edition pieces have perhaps been more significant in extending the reach of artwear to a wider audience than the one-of-a-kind work.[19]

Some artists have found production a satisfying way to make a living from their art, others have gone into production for a time, then abandoned it, and some have chosen to avoid it entirely because it does not interest them or perhaps because the nature of their work—Candace Kling's intricately folded ribbon headdresses, or Norma Minkowitz's fine-grained crochet, for example—does not lend itself to multiples (2.28). Among those in production, Marian Clayden has probably been the most commercially successful. Her work comes as close to fashion design as wearable art gets, and she herself finds artistic fulfillment in designing clothes and the textiles they are made from, which are custom-woven for her and hand-dyed under her direction (2.26). Nonetheless, some of her colleagues were horrified when she decided to open her business, feeling perhaps that it was a betrayal of her art or the anti-fashion ethos.[20] Tim Harding, who also has a very successful production business, has succeeded in carving out the space to continue making major art pieces alongside his line of production coats. The New York–based knitter Linda Mendelson has managed to do the same, as has Santa Fe–based knitter Susan Summa (2.32). Carter Smith, a prolific dyer who for many years sold his cloth to fashion designers like Halston, now prefers turning it into a limited line of dresses himself rather than selling it as yardage to others (2.27).[21]

For every successful artist engaged in artwear production, however, there is another who became bored or disenchanted, either with the demands of running a business, which greatly reduced their opportunity for creative work, or with the watering-down of their ideas necessitated by the demands of the market. Jean Williams Cacicedo and Ana Lisa Hedstrom, for example, both had very successful production businesses and both chose to walk away, Hedstrom in 1992 and Cacicedo in 1998.

1990s: Retrenchment and Change

The early 1990s was a difficult time for artwear in the United States. Recession hit luxury markets, including art, studio craft, and high fashion, extremely hard. The fashion aesthetic changed from the broad-shouldered, wedge-shaped or waisted silhouette of the 1980s that easily accommodated wearable art's unstructured shapes to a far more slender, body-conscious line and a fondness for exposed skin. Some of the most gifted artists, many of whom had been working in this genre for fifteen or twenty years, moved on to studio fiber, to other art media, or out of art altogether, and relatively few young artists emerged to take their places. Fashion magazines regularly highlighted new designers who were creating one-of-a-kind or limited-edition handmade, hand-embroidered, -dyed, or -painted clothing, but the designers were identifying themselves with fashion, not with wearable art. Teacher/artist Jo Ann Stabb foretold some of these problems in 1988, suggesting that the genre was no longer in step with a technology-mad younger generation eager to create with computers, and that many of the artists and the art had gone stale.[22] As the 1990s progressed, galleries and dealers began to disappear: Jacqueline Lippetz in Chicago, Bunny Horowitz in Florida, and Wittenborn & Hollingsworth in Los Angeles all closed; Joanne Rapp in Scottsdale, Arizona, sold The Hand and the Spirit and its new owner moved away from wearable art. The market crash in 2000 brought yet another round of shrinkage. Most devastating was the closing of Obiko and the boutique at Bergdorf's upon Sandra Sakata's untimely death in 1997, which affected artwear on both coasts.

Nonetheless, artwear has maintained its presence. Some of its original leaders, like Cacicedo, Hedstrom, and Clayden, are still working, and others, like Lipkin who stopped making wearables in the early 1990s, have recently returned to it. Many artists are still involved in production and, despite all those that closed, a number of galleries have remained. Julie Schafler Dale, faced in 1998 with the choice of closing or moving her gallery, moved to a larger space. On the West Coast, Monique Zhang, who formerly worked at Obiko, started a successor gallery called Cicada in 1998, the year after Sakata's death, which has attempted to fill the hole left by Obiko's closure; and Widney Moore opened a wearable art gallery in Portland, Oregon, in 2000.

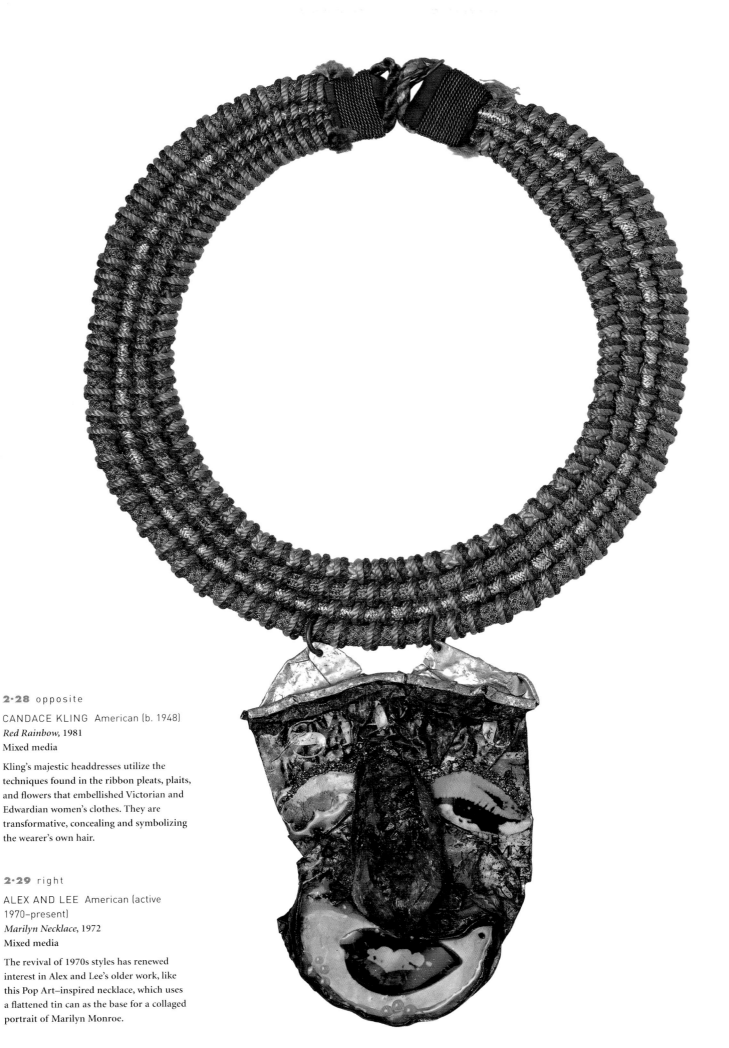

2·28 opposite

CANDACE KLING American (b. 1948)
Red Rainbow, 1981
Mixed media

Kling's majestic headdresses utilize the techniques found in the ribbon pleats, plaits, and flowers that embellished Victorian and Edwardian women's clothes. They are transformative, concealing and symbolizing the wearer's own hair.

2·29 right

ALEX AND LEE American (active 1970–present)
Marilyn Necklace, 1972
Mixed media

The revival of 1970s styles has renewed interest in Alex and Lee's older work, like this Pop Art–inspired necklace, which uses a flattened tin can as the base for a collaged portrait of Marilyn Monroe.

2·30 top

JUSTINE LIMPUS PARISH American (b. 1951)

Nouveau Renaissance, 2001

Silk satin, organza; block- and digital inkjet-printed, painted, shibori-dyed, pleated

Parish makes artwear professionally and also participates in competitions like the Bernina Fashion Show, for which this piece was made. Its pleated gown suggests Fortuny's Delphos dresses, and the cape's peacock-feather motif is associated with Liberty's.

2.31 above

Artwear from the American southwest, which this ikat-dyed cotton coat by Deborah Hughes Zane epitomizes, often reflects the Hispanic and Native American influences and colors of the region.

The Santa Fe Weaving Gallery, which began as an artists' collective in the 1970s and became a dedicated wearable art gallery representing small producers in the 1980s (2.31), was purchased in 1992 by Jill Heppenheimer and Barbara Lanning, who have brought both a deep appreciation of the genre and considerable business experience to the field. They have expanded their gallery's reach and sought, through advertising, teaching, networking, and an annual conference, to increase support for established artists and help identify and mentor emerging ones. Museums large and small, like the Textile Museum in Washington, D.C., which mounted the major retrospective *The Kimono Inspiration* in 1996, have continued to pay serious attention, and there is evidence that artwear's presence in museum permanent collections is growing. New, nongallery outlets have also emerged. In 1996 artist Susan Summa organized Atelier, a thrice-yearly wholesale show in New York that coincides with the presentation of the city's ready-to-wear collections, to bring wearable art in closer proximity to fashion buyers.[23] At Atelier, artwear artists (characterized as artisans, the term with which the fashion world currently seems most comfortable) who focus on cloth and on artistic self-expression rub shoulders with fashion designers who are focused on current trends and fit, and avant-garde designers, who focus on edgy experimentation, perhaps using traditional materials in contemporary ways or vice versa; it is a microcosm of three major design approaches to clothing. And a sweet, if likely temporary, development is that the 1970s revival that has preoccupied fashion since the late 1990s has brought the artwear of the early years back into fashion as reinterpreted styles and as vintage clothing (2.29).

The Amateur Audience

A large and enthusiastic amateur audience for wearable art has developed since the 1970s. Some artists find the support and interest very positive; others fear that the uneven quality of the amateur work jeopardizes the standing of the genre. Textile crafts as leisure activities for educated, middle-class American women have been on the rise since the 1940s, when a number of the handweavers' guilds were established.[24] During the same period quilting and embroidery, which have been popular forms of leisure needlework for centuries, also occasioned the formation of guilds of aficionados, and during the 1980s artwear began to spawn its own guilds scattered across the United States. The women who use these pastimes to make art to wear may be doing so because they are drawn to that form of creative expression, or because they are looking for alternatives to the clothes the fashion industry is offering them. Many also make wearable art specifically for competitions and exhibitions. There are dozens of such shows staged annually at conferences, fairs, and shows all across the United States; most are juried. Since 1979, the Fairfield Fashion Show (renamed the Bernina Fashion Show in 2001 when its sponsorship changed) has been at the pinnacle. Bernina is an invitational wearable art show staged in conjunction with the International Quilt Festival in Houston, Texas, each fall. Between forty and fifty entrants, most involved professionally in quilting, fabric, or dressmaking, are invited to participate each year. Most entries incorporate traditional quilt-making techniques—quilting, piecing, or appliqué—but usually they also feature a wide variety of other surface design techniques. Three winners are awarded prizes, and all entries are photographed for a publication and subsequently tour throughout the country.

Although artists occasionally cross over (2.30), the wearable art of the guilds and juried shows is largely a separate world from that of the major galleries, museums, department stores, and limited-edition designers, despite the large amount of promotion and exposure it receives. The work is heavily influenced by processes taught by the major artists in the field and many of the more prominent amateurs in classes and workshops. The multitude of how-to books and instructional videos that have been published since 1970 have also been a rich source of information, offering guidance on every possible textile technique from basic quilting to making ribbon flowers inspired by the trimming on nineteenth-century costumes. Artists like quilter Yvonne Porcella have developed successful publishing careers as authors of series of books based on their work, and have garnered large followings (2.33).

Fashion and Artwear

Wearable art may have positioned itself in opposition to fashion in the 1970s but the two have been moving inexorably closer ever since. It is fair to say that artwear is now a recognizable style within fashion. Many artists feel that some wearable art has been copied by fashion designers who have essentially capitalized unfairly on others' ideas, but in most cases this is difficult to prove. Fashion does tend to vacuum up great swaths of visual and cultural information; but, in my view, although fashion has certainly absorbed and used the aspects of wearable art it found interesting, it has rarely resorted to outright copying.[25] In its turn, artwear has taken what it has wished and needed from fashion.

Since the eighteenth century, Western culture has conceived of fashion as an inherently feminine pursuit that is frivolous and ephemeral, "women's work" at its least admirable. This is one of the primary reasons why wearable art sought its distance from fashion and why it has struggled with their inevitable fusion. Both fashion and artwear have been eager to ally themselves with art, which is accorded high status in Western culture. Artwear adopted the Arts and Crafts model of creating art through exploration and mastery of materials and technique. Fashion's approach was to adopt and co-opt imagery and other aspects of fine art, and it has been doing so since at least the middle of the nineteenth century when early couturiers, Charles Frederick Worth in particular, began to take pains to associate themselves and their work with the art world.[26] Worth attracted clients with custom-designed textiles and fashions modeled on images drawn from sixteenth-, seventeenth-, and eighteenth-

2.32 above

SUSAN SUMMA American (b. 1948)
Tunic, ca. 1984
Loom-knitted cotton

Summa, originally a weaver, gravitated to machine knitting because it was a better way for her to render complex imagery.

YVONNE PORCELLA American (b. 1936)
Pasha on the 10:04, 1984
Cotton; pieced, painted, quilted

This kimono appeared on the cover of one of Porcella's instructional books. *Pasha* is the title of its commercially printed lining fabric; Porcella, who hand-painted the single colorful figure, imagined her as a lady of the evening riding the rails "to somewhere or nowhere."

2.34 – 2.35 below

Clothes like Saint Laurent's 1985 evening jacket based on Van Gogh's *Irises* and Blass's 1988 Matisse-inspired counterpart can extend fine art's high status to both designer and wearer. The Blass photo connects art and couture explicitly via a prop chair, which echoes the chair embroidered on the jacket, set astride a heavy gold frame.

century paintings in his own and other private and public collections.[27] Many of his successors, including Madeleine Vionnet, Elsa Schiaparelli, Yves Saint Laurent, and Vivienne Westwood, have used fine art as a rich library of ideas and source material, as a framework for shaping their own design philosophies, and as an excellent marketing tool.

It seemed to become more important to fashion to classify itself as art during the contemporary art boom periods of the 1980s and 90s. Calling a fashion designer an artist is perhaps the ultimate tribute, suggesting that his or her work has extraordinary creativity and cultural importance, that it will transcend its commercial origins and have a lasting impact on society. Garments with a recognizable connection to art offer their wearers the opportunity literally to wrap themselves in an aura of cultural awareness, refinement, and superiority, and to ally themselves variously with an aristocratic European past, with cutting-edge Modernism, or, more recently, with popular culture. In the nineteenth and early twentieth centuries, the art connection made couture deeply attractive to aristocrats looking for new ways to express status sartorially and to the upwardly mobile new rich looking to establish themselves socially. Despite the shift in class distinctions since World War II, these have remained powerful considerations in the dance between art and fashion.

One of the ways in which fashion has embraced art has muddied the public's understanding of what wearable art is. Since the 1960s, fashion designers, encouraged

2·36 top

In 1986, *Harper's Bazaar* promoted this commercially produced wool and metallic sweater, which it dubbed "wearable art." The sweater bears a licensed image by Erté that originally appeared as the April 1930 cover.

2.37 above

Sculptor and performance artist Jacqueline Matisse Monnier wears her *Moon Pieces* caftan, which was made from yardage she designed in 1981 in collaboration with the Fabric Workshop and Museum in Philadelphia.

2.38 opposite

DESIGNER UNKNOWN, AFTER ANDY WARHOL

The Souper Dress, ca. 1968

Printed cellulose and cotton

Recalling Warhol's *Campbell's Soup* silkscreens, this mass-produced dress neatly appropriated the master-appropriator's work for the mass-market.

no doubt by Pop Art, have periodically plastered imagery appropriated from specific paintings and graphic works across their clothes. Yves Saint Laurent's 1965 Mondrian collection was one of the first, and most famous, of such borrowings. Saint Laurent later repeated his Mondrian success with salutes first to Picasso (1979) and then to Surrealism (1984), and van Gogh and Braque (1988) (2.34). Jean-Charles de Castelbajac in 1984 and Gianni Versace in 1990 reprised Warhol, Castelbajac "did" da Vinci in 1988, while in 1986 Paco Rabanne reimaged sections of a canvas by the seventeenth-century artist Georges de la Tour across a group of four hand-painted and sequined evening gowns. These were adaptations, of course, not slavish copies, and they may be seasoned with humor or ironic self-awareness; but they are also appropriations of the status associated with each work of art by the designer and the wearer. This painterly imagery is not always an unqualified success when translated from the canvas to surface design on the body. An article by Amy Fine Collins comparing Saint Laurent's jacket based on van Gogh's *Irises* with Bill Blass's jacket based on Matisse's paintings of Nice interiors comments that Saint Laurent's adaptation of van Gogh's floral imagery and technique was rather more skillful than Blass's Matisse reproductions, which had architectural details ending up in odd places on the wearer's body (2.35).[28]

During this same period the middle-class hunger for a piece of the art world was also satisfied by art as surface design on clothing, and at times this has also been dubbed *wearable art* by the media. The Warhol-inspired Campbell's Soup paper dress of ca. 1968 may be the first example (2.38); it was followed during the art boom of the 1980s by a raft of readily available limited-edition clothing at a wide range of prices that sported imagery drawn from art originally created in other media by well-established artists. Many were living artists who were licensing their work to manufacturers; graffiti artist Keith Haring also opened his own retail outlet. One article entitled "Wearable Art," published in *Harper's Bazaar* in 1986, featured the then-94-year-old Erté's 1930 illustration for a *Bazaar* cover re-created as a wool and metallic sweater (2.36), a jacket by Haring, and a suit made from a textile designed by David Hockney that the magazine described as "a truly wearable masterpiece."[29] The practice has remained

popular, with both living artists and the estates of famous dead ones like Picasso and Warhol licensing their work for reproduction on clothing. Although it is confusing that the term *wearable art* has been applied to these clothes, since they do not conform to the definition of wearable art as artist-made clothes created from handmade textiles and seem to have been conceived of as fashion, the phenomenon is analogous to the distribution of engravings of famous paintings to the middle classes in earlier centuries. It is a way of spreading the culture and appreciation of art—perhaps the ultimate absorption by society of art that may once have been regarded as impossibly avant-garde.

Artists have also actively collaborated with fashion designers many times over the past century. Madeleine Vionnet worked in the 1920s with the Futurist painter and illustrator Thayaht (Ernesto Michaelles) (2.40), and Elsa Schiaparelli famously collaborated with Surrealists Salvador Dalí and Jean Cocteau in the late 1930s. Italian artist Lucio Fontana created designs for Milanese dressmaker Bini-Talese in 1961. In the 1990s, Issey Miyake collaborated with a number of artists in the production of his *Pleats Please* series (2.39), and Gianni Versace commissioned designs for printed textiles from Julian Schnabel and Jim Dine.[30] These were image- and not process-oriented collaborations created for mainstream fashion, and as such sit just outside the realm of artwear; but artists have also created designs for one-of-a-kind and limited-edition wearable clothing with process more in mind.

The Fabric Workshop was founded in Philadelphia in 1977 with the dual purpose of giving contemporary artists who customarily work in other media the opportunity to explore designing for yardage and training young people in textile printing techniques. The artists collaborate with the Workshop's master printers and apprentices in the execution of their designs, although inevitably much of the technical work is done by the staff. Many fine artists find it liberating to create art in a completely new medium; for some, the residency at the Workshop is also the first time they make art that is functional. None of them seem to abandon their primary media as a result, but it is likely that these experiences color their subsequent work.[31] Most, though not all, of the garments produced at the Workshop are

2·39 right

ISSEY MIYAKE Japanese (b. 1938)
Pleats Please: Guest Artist #1, 1996
Polyester; pleated and printed

Miyake's Fortuny-like pleated polyester garments first appeared in 1988, and he has collaborated with others to push the visual boundaries of the material. This enigmatic dress is the result of a collaboration with artist Yasumasa Morimura.

2·40 opposite

MADELEINE VIONNET
French (1876–1975)
Evening Dress, ca. 1924
Silk crepe embroidered with opalescent glass beads

Vionnet likely designed this dress in collaboration with the Futurist artist Thayaht, who created textiles, clothes, and jewelry for Vionnet et Cie. in the late 1910s and 20s.

wearable; indeed, the artists are often photographed wearing them (2.37), and multiples are usually produced, albeit in very limited numbers. A similar experiment undertaken in 1982 by Crown Point Press, a fine-art press in San Francisco that specialized in etching, was less successful. Kathan Brown, the press's founder, was eager to explore different printing processes and media, including screenprint on silk. She invited interested artists to contribute works to be hand-printed on silk kimonos, jackets, robes, and pajamas (2.41). Her invitation netted fifteen artists, including several who either had previously or would subsequently be artists-in-residence at the Fabric Workshop (2.42). Perhaps because the artists were not offered the kind of expert guidance in textile design provided at the Fabric Workshop, not all of the garments were wholly successful. Moreover, they proved extremely expensive to produce, and Brown lacked the necessary connections to market clothing. As a result, the project was swiftly abandoned.

One of the most significant links between fashion and artwear has been the move of shibori-dyed fabrics from one-of-a-kind and production artwear into the fashion industry during the past thirty years.[32] Shibori-dyers in the United States, Europe, Asia, and India have teamed up with fashion designers, many of them small producers, but also some major names with the power to bring shibori to a wide audience. This has been going on in the United States since the early 1970s when dyers like Carter Smith began producing shibori-dyed fabric in quantity for fashion designers like Halston. Yoshiko Wada helped to facilitate this trend internationally when, during a year-long residency in India in 1983, she introduced textile designer Asha Sarabhai to Issey Miyake. Sarabhai was on a quest to save *bandhani*, a traditional Indian form of bound-resist-dyeing, by employing local artisans in her native India to produce her designs, and the meeting with Miyake led to a line of Indian-inspired and -made clothes for the Japanese market.[33] More recently, fashion designers have been commissioning shibori textiles—Paco Rabanne, for instance, in 1992 from artist Hélène Soubeyran, and both Yohji Yamamoto and Hiroko Koshino from Kaei Hayakawa, who learned *arashi* shibori from Reiichi Suzuki, the last surviving traditional *arashi* artisan.[34]

A number of fashion designers also design their own textiles—Emilio Pucci, Michael Vollbracht, and Zandra Rhodes, for instance. Rhodes, trained as a textile designer, started her business in the 1960s and has some common ground with artwear. Many of her early garments were drawn from the models in Max Tilke's book *Costume Patterns and Designs*, also a guide for those who make wearable art, and her use of ethnic garments and willingness to flout convention in her work was an inspiration for many of them (2.43). The Dutch-born, New York–based Koos van den Akker, who started his business in New York in 1968, is probably the Western designer whose process and aesthetics are most like those of wearable art. He has described his work as painting with fabric.[35] In fact, what he creates is collage, a profligate layering of color on color and pattern on pattern, often using fabrics that are, or look, handmade, and which he turns into one-of-a-kind fashions. His work can recall that of any one of several artwear artists, depending on the piece, and it serves as a model for many of the amateurs.[36] He has not credited wearable

art as an influence, but it is perhaps not coincidental that for a number of years in the 1970s and 1980s, his workroom and store was on Madison Avenue only a few blocks away from the Artisans' Gallery.

Issey Miyake started his business in 1970, when wearable art was emerging, and he is probably the fashion designer with whom it has most in common philosophically, even though he designs for a mass audience. From the start, his work has been completely grounded both in traditional Japanese (i.e. nonfashion) garments and philosophy, and in his textiles (2.44). He does not make his own textiles, but his thirty-year collaboration with designer Makiko Minagawa has produced revolutionary fabrics that have had tremendous influence on his garments and have placed his work on a fashion plane of its own. Miyake's textiles characteristically mix traditional processes with new technology and materials like polyester. That same amazing fusion of art and technology can also be found in the work of designer Yoshiki Hishinuma who, unlike Miyake, creates his own textiles (2.45).[37]

2·41 opposite

WILLIAM T. WILEY American (b. 1937)
Mr. and Mrs. Casual in Smoothasilk, 1982
Screenprinted silk charmeuse

This robe is a rare piece of wearable art created by a noted painter and printmaker. His use of natural imagery, though rendered in his characteristic, cartoonlike style, aligns him with many others making artwear.

2·42 below

ROBERT KUSHNER American (b. 1949)
Jacket, 1982
Screenprinted silk charmeuse

Kushner's earlier, fashion-inflected performance art, his participation in the Pattern and Decoration movement, and his long-time interest in textiles led him to create one of the more successful of the Crown Point Press wearable artworks. Kushner also created artwear at the Fabric Workshop.

2·43 right

ZANDRA RHODES British (b. 1940)
Caftan-style Dress of "Knitted Circle" Print, 1969

Rhodes, a textile designer by training, was a
strong influence on wearable art. Her iconoclastic approach to fashion, use of ethnic
garment forms, and self-designed fabric
encouraged many artists to experiment.
Like many who made artwear, Rhodes was
influenced by sources like Max Tilke's book
Costume Patterns and Designs.

2·44 below

ISSEY MIYAKE Japanese (b. 1938)
Paradise Lost, 1977
Printed silk

Like much artwear, Miyake's work fuses
Eastern and Western elements. The design for
this coat, a square into which sleeves have been
set, derived from the kimono tradition, while
the image on the back, by Japanese graphic
artist Tadanori Yokoo, references Milton's
Paradise Lost.

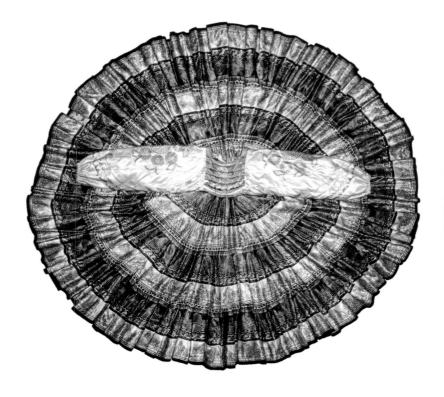

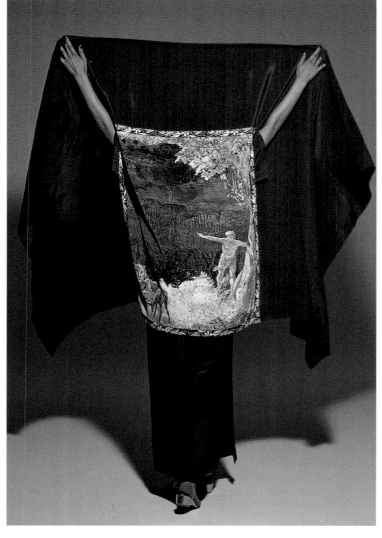

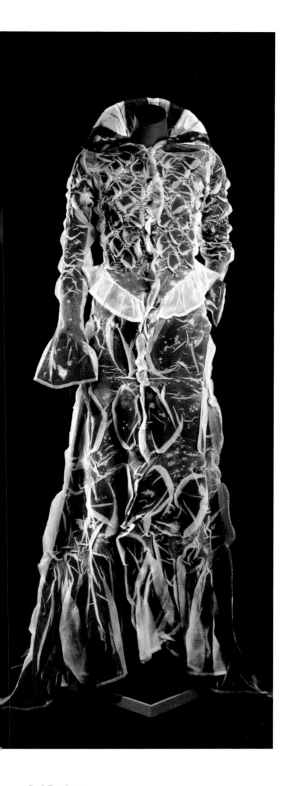

The early 1970s revival in fashion over the last few years has sparked a lot of interest in early wearable art. Nicolas Ghesquière, the designer for the venerable French couture house Balenciaga, created a 1970s revival collection for spring 2002 inspired, he claimed, by the work of Koos van den Akker. It featured a vest that was an uncredited, virtually line-for-line copy of one created by Kaisik Wong and published in 1974 in the book *Native Funk and Flash* (2.46, 2.47). An intern at the online fashion site *Hintmag* recognized the vest, and the site chose to publicize what Ghesquière had done. The story received considerable attention from the mainstream press and Ghesquière, nonchalant at first about the copying, later apologized.[38] Designers inevitably look for visual inspiration from a wide variety of sources, but this appears to be the first example of a designer simply recontextualizing a specific artwear garment into high fashion. The ethics of such direct copying aside, the incident had the unexpected benefit of thrusting more of the artwear of that period into the fashion limelight, and fashion seemed to like what it saw. Cameron Silver, owner of the vintage clothing store Decades in Los Angeles, who had independently decided to mount a special show and sale of some of Kaisik Wong's work shortly before the *Hintmag* story broke, became enamored of wearable art, and ended up taking a collection of pieces from the 1970s and 80s to Barney's in New York for a one-time special sale. As recently as summer 2003, *Hintmag* was touting the Art Fiend Foundation in New York as part of "a growing movement to revive the late 60s and 70s taste for wearable art."[39]

2·46 - 2·47 below

Kaisik Wong's collaged vest (top), published in *Native Funk and Flash* in 1974, was the inspiration for Nicolas Ghesquière's vest for his spring 2002 Balenciaga collection (bottom). Copying and revivalism are long-established aspects of the fashion design process, but Ghesquière's vest follows Wong's so closely that it sparked a brief wave of media attention focused on issues of plagiarism in fashion.

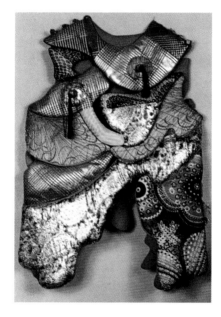

2.45 above

YOSHIKI HISHINUMA Japanese (b. 1958)
Evening Gown, Fish, 1997
Heat transfer on polyester

Hishinuma created this amazing dress by drawing both on eighteenth-century French fashion and on the concepts of shibori (shaped resist-dyeing), which he applied to a special polyester fabric that shrinks when it is heated. The dress's three-dimensional, fish-scalelike pattern was made using a wooden mold, to which the polyester was secured before it was shrunk.

3 Models, Methods, and Meanings

INA KOZEL working in U.S.
(b. Lithuania, 1944)
Our Lady of Rather Deep Waters, 1985
Silk; wax-resist-painted, color Xerox transfer,
painted expanding foam plastic

Water is a frequent theme of Kozel's, reinforced
by the watery effect she achieves with her
painting technique.

Learning from Japan

For a number of reasons, Japan emerged from
the multiethnic swirl of sources as the one
with the greatest impact on artwear. As Nancy
Corwin has described, the West experienced
a new wave of Japonisme after World War II
that was especially influential on crafts and
design.[1] By the 1970s, Japanese techniques and
aesthetics were being emulated by a number
of American textile artists, and the Japanese
tradition of reverence for crafts that had so
impressed the artists of the Arts and Crafts
movement was not lost on this new generation
of Americans, who longed to be accorded the
same respect and status. Many other non-
Western cultures do not separate art and craft,
but Japan is a First World country, whose
sophisticated urban art and craft have historically
been highly valued by the West. China has
had similar standing in Western art, but
contemporary Japan was open to the West in
the 1970s in a way that China was not and its
characteristic methods for figuring textiles
included processes that were more hospitable
to artwear. Japanese craftsmanship has been
developed to an extremely high level, and, as
a result of Japan's own postindustrial craft
revival that began in the late 1920s,[2] textile craft
skills were preserved and collections of folk
textiles assembled both in Japan and in the
United States.[3] In the 1970s, these skills could be
acquired both through apprenticeship and in art
schools, and it was possible for non-Japanese
artists, such as John Marshall and Ina Kozel
(3.1, 3.6), to study these crafts formally in Japan.

Japanese émigrés, most crucially Yoshiko Wada
as discussed in Chapter 2, also taught in America
and subsequently around the world, bringing
Japanese craft techniques to the attention of
a wide audience. As we have seen, artists also
valued Japanese clothing, particularly the
kimono, as a conceptual mediator between two-
dimensional textiles and three-dimensional
garments, quite separate from the specifics of its
cut and construction and regardless of whether
it conformed to Japanese tradition or had been
modified to correspond more closely to Western
ideas of fit.[4] Indeed, the kimono has become so
ubiquitous that it has tended to obscure the
other ethnic garments that have also been used
as models.

Techniques and Materials

The creation of textiles is central to artwear;
in most cases the textile, not the construction
of the garment, is the locus of the art. It is
significant that many makers of artwear
originally trained in nontextile media like
painting; most came to this type of art because
they were seduced by its materials and
techniques, and they remain driven by their
passion for textiles.

Virtually every major process used to
structure, color, and figure textiles has been
pressed into service for wearable art: weaving,
knitting, dyeing, printing, painting, felting,
piecing, appliqué, embroidery. Artists will often
go to unorthodox lengths in their experiments
with process; Marian Clayden once attempted
to pattern a textile by burning it in her sandwich

3·2 previous page

DINA KNAPP American (b. 1947)
See It Like a Native, History Kimono #1, 1982
Cotton, polyester, plastic, paper; painted,
appliquéd, Xerox-transferred, printed,
assembled

Newspaper and magazine pictures of early
1980s events in Florida form the coat's
imagery. The sunny tourist associations of
Florida with flamingoes and palm trees are
countered by images of protest marches, war
planes, guns, and Haitian refugees.

3.3 above

TIM HARDING American (b. 1950)
Oaks, 1988
Cotton; free-reverse appliqué (collage-
layered, quilted, slashed, frayed)

This painterly landscape is rendered in reverse
appliqué, in which one or more layers of cloth
are slashed or cut away to reveal a contrasting
color beneath. It is Harding's signature
technique, and the foundation of his very
distinctive style.

3.4 above

CARTER SMITH American (b. 1946)
Origin of Shibori, 1986–87
Silk; shibori-dyed

Smith's fascination with and pleasure in the
dyeing process have driven him to endless,
complex experimentation with methods and
materials; he is one of the pioneers of shibori-
dyeing in the United States and one of its
most technically innovative practitioners.

JACQUELYN ROESCH-SANCHEZ
American (b. 1946)
Janet's Kimono, 1981
Loom-knitted rayon

To a Western eye, this short modified
kimono resembles a cardigan. Sanchez's
work is about color and her garments
are spectrums, sometimes incorporating
more than one hundred different shades of
commercially dyed rayon. *Janet's Kimono*
has thirty-five.

3·6 opposite bottom

JOHN MARSHALL American (b. 1955)
Phoenix, 1981
Japanese silk wedding jacquard; *tsutsugaki*
(rice-paste resist)

Marshall studied dollmaking in Japan before
segueing to artwear, and Japan is a particularly
strong influence on his work. This coat's
silk fabric is woven with phoenixes, which
suggested the dyed imagery that overlays
them.

toaster[5] and Tim Harding has confessed to
shooting a piece of cloth to see what the effect
would be.[6] Artists often stake out aesthetic
territory through technique, like the knitter
Linda Mendelson, the painter Ina Kozel, the dyer
Carter Smith, and the king of reverse-appliqué
Tim Harding, all of whom have cleaved to a
primary technique that they have explored fully
throughout their careers and used to develop
an instantly recognizable style (3.3, 3.4). More
often, artists combine different structural
and/or decorative techniques for their signatures
and may, like Katherine Westphal and Jean
Williams Cacicedo, push the limits of one
process until they feel they have exhausted its
possibilities and then move on to something
new (3.10). Artists have also relied on and
utilized a wide array of modern technologies
and commercially produced materials in the
creation of their handmade textiles—weavers,
crocheters, and knitters may use commercially

produced yarns; dyers, printers, and painters
more often choose synthetic than natural dyes,
which they may apply to commercially made
fabric (3.9). There are artists who use only
natural fibers and artists who prefer to use
synthetics, for ideological as well as practical
reasons; but for many, the question of whether
the physical properties of the material and its
cultural or emotional associations will allow
them to create the textile they envision is the
more important consideration. So, for example,
wool is central to the work of artists like
Cacicedo and Jorie Johnson, who make and
manipulate felt; leather to the work of Jane
Kosminsky, who has a deep connection with
primitive art and reptilian imagery (3.7);
synthetics to Ellen Hauptli for her work based
on permanent pleating (3.13); and silk to a
whole host of dyers for its affinity to brilliant
color, its tactile and draping qualities, and also
its high status.

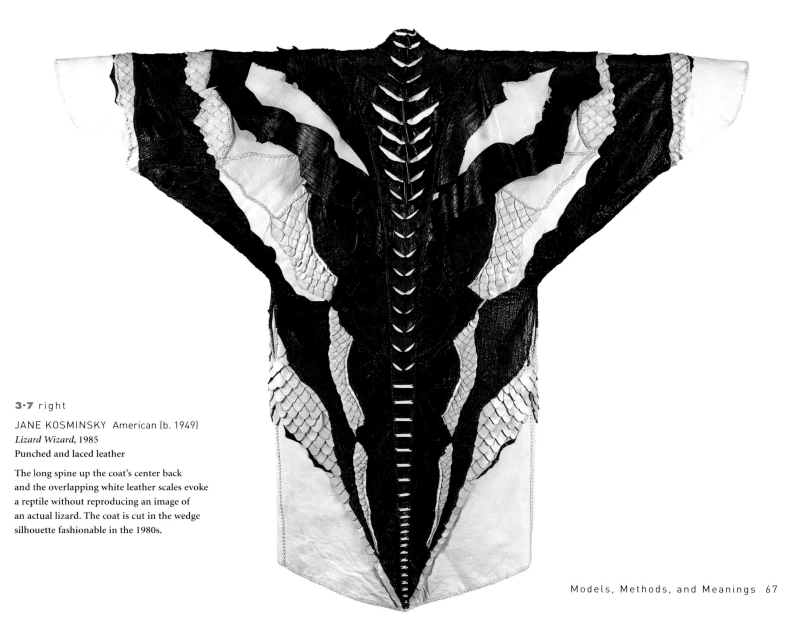

3·7 right

JANE KOSMINSKY American (b. 1949)
Lizard Wizard, 1985
Punched and laced leather

The long spine up the coat's center back
and the overlapping white leather scales evoke
a reptile without reproducing an image of
an actual lizard. The coat is cut in the wedge
silhouette fashionable in the 1980s.

3.8 above

INA KOZEL working in U.S.
(b. Lithuania, 1944)
Robe from the Red Sea, 1988
Silk; wax-resist painted

Kozel uses *roketsuzome*, a Japanese technique in which fabric sections are painted with hot wax, which resists applications of dye. Each color is resisted separately; for a complex image Kozel might go through the process a dozen or more times before removing the wax and steaming the silk to set the dyes.

3.9 left

ROSE KELLY American (b. 1955)
Longjohns, 1987
Painted cotton

Kelly often paints or prints on ready-made garments, as she did with her longjohns series. The motifs, which reflect African, Native American, and Maori influences, resemble body paint or tattoo, which was just beginning to appear on fashion's radar in the late 1980s.

3.10 opposite

JEAN WILLIAMS CACICEDO
American (b. 1948)
Pink Petals, 1978
Hand- and loom-knitted wool; dyed, pieced, appliquéd

Cacicedo has explored several different techniques in the course of her long career. This jacket marks her transition from crochet, in which she had been working since the late 1960s, to knitting.

Artwear has also made use of less usual materials when the content of a piece has warranted it: the range has included paper, plastic, cork, wood, printed circuit boards, shredded currency (3.16), and a wide variety of found and recycled objects (3.11, 3.12, 3.15, 3.24). Artists making wearables are also perfectly willing to employ an arsenal of commercial and high-tech tools like pleaters, knitting machines, airbrushes, photocopiers, dye sublimation printers, and computers in creating handmade textiles, increasing their sophistication as technology has advanced over the past thirty years (3.17, 3.18). So the idea of making cloth "by hand" should not be taken to mean "without modern technology." Indeed, new tools can be as important as rediscovered techniques in keeping artists engaged with their media and their technologically savvy audiences.

A few techniques, especially crochet, are associated with specific eras in artwear. Crochet remained popular among artists like Janet Lipkin, Sharron Hedges, and Dina Knapp until the late 1970s (3.20). It offered a number of advantages: the technique was quick to learn, it made garments that could stretch to fit (a boon to those with no dressmaking experience), and the basic stitch, which produced a long chain of fabric, allowed artists as yet unused to textiles to feel as if they were drawing on the body with yarn and to create any kind of motif they wanted, from vaguely amoebalike forms to convincing representational images of nature. Its chunky texture also suited the period's fashions and desire for the obviously handmade, although it was also used by artists such as Norma Minkowitz to create garments of great textural subtlety and sophistication (3.19). Changes in fashionable tastes in the late 1970s coincided with the desire of many artists to produce work faster, either themselves or as part of small design businesses engaged in production, and many crocheters gravitated to knitting machines (3.14).[7] With the machines, artists could not only make art more quickly, they could knit far more complex representational imagery, like that found on Janet Lipkin's *Nudes* coat (1992) (1.1), or the text that adorns much of Linda Mendelson's work

(3.21). Knitting in fine metal, a technique pioneered by Arline Fisch, has also characterized the work of some jewelry artists who have used it to create garments like collars, cuffs, hats, or gloves that cross over into artwear territory (3.24, 3.25).

Handweaving was one of the first methods used by textile artists in this era to make clothing, as is attested by a tunic woven by renowned fiber artist and teacher Trude Guermonprez in 1958.[8] This tunic can be seen as a rare tangible link between artwear and the Bauhaus since Guermonprez, though not educated there herself, trained in Germany under Bauhäusler Benita Otte and subsequently taught at Black Mountain College with Anni Albers. The majority of wearable art hand-wovens are figured in geometric motifs and many explore the Bauhausian realms of color, form, and texture (3.26, 3.27). Weaving boasts distinguished practitioners like Randall Darwall and Deborah Valoma, but overall it has lagged behind other techniques in popularity. This is in contrast to the tremendous popularity of weaving among studio fiber artists making non-wearables. This may be due in part to weaving's time-consuming nature relative to other processes that utilize ready-made fabric; it may also be attributable to artwear's strong focus on surface design, which may attract fewer people interested in achieving surface through structure. Many artists who make wearable art certainly have learned to weave, but often choose to make their clothing using other methods. Like crochet, weaving tends to be more associated with wearable art's 1970s counterculture phase than its sleeker, graphic 80s phase; and many who began as weavers, like Victoria Rabinowe, have ended up moving on to other techniques over time. It is also possible that there are political reasons. In the hierarchy of the textile arts world, those who make artwear have complained of feeling that they rank below the studio fiber artists, just as tapestry ranks above costume in the art world in general. By choosing to avoid one of studio fiber art's most characteristic processes, some artists may, consciously or not, be attempting to establish and defend their own unique artwear territory.

MARIO RIVOLI American (b. 1943)
Mexican Jacket, 1989
Cotton, buttons, found objects; assemblage

On the back of the jacket, a Mexican couple clad in traditional dress emerges from a sea of buttons and ruffles.

3.12 above

ESTELLE AKAMINE American (b. 1954)
Typewriter Ribbon Dress, 1993
Computer printer ribbon, nylon, foam; loom-woven

Akamine's longtime interest in using recycled materials in her textiles and clothing led her to the artist-in-residence program at San Francisco's dump, where she collected, cleaned, and processed a wide variety of discarded materials into clothing for San Francisco's elegant annual Black-and-White Ball.

3·13 below

ELLEN HAUPTLI American (b. 1949)
Evening ensemble, 1977
Pleated polyester

This pleated ensemble recalls Mariano
Fortuny's work, but in fact Hauptli's
introduction to the sculptural qualities of
pleats, which became her signature process
and with which she has experimented
endlessly, came when she restored an antique
Chinese jacket with pleated sides for an
exhibition in the late 1970s.

3.14 opposite

MARIKA CONTOMPASIS American
(b. 1948)
Wedding Ensemble, 1972
Loom-knitted and crocheted hand-dyed wool,
embroidery

This was an early loom-knitted piece for
Contompasis who, at the time, was better
known for crochet. Contompasis colored
the wool with natural dyestuffs in tribute
to the bride's profession as an herbalist.

3·15 above

MARK MAHALL American (1949–1978)
Safety-Pin Jacket, 1978
Mixed media

Mahall's glistening meditation on pattern and
texture, created by sticking a commercial vinyl
bomber jacket with thousands of brass safety
pins, could also be read as golden armor for
a modern-day hero, or a gentler, wearable-art
version of Punk fashion.

3·16 opposite

CAT CHOW American (b. 1973)
Not For Sale, 2002
Currency, fishing line, glue

This fashionable fitted gown is constructed
of a thousand shredded dollar bills donated
by a thousand sponsors. George Washington's
face can be spotted peeking out from the
center front, center back, and side seams.

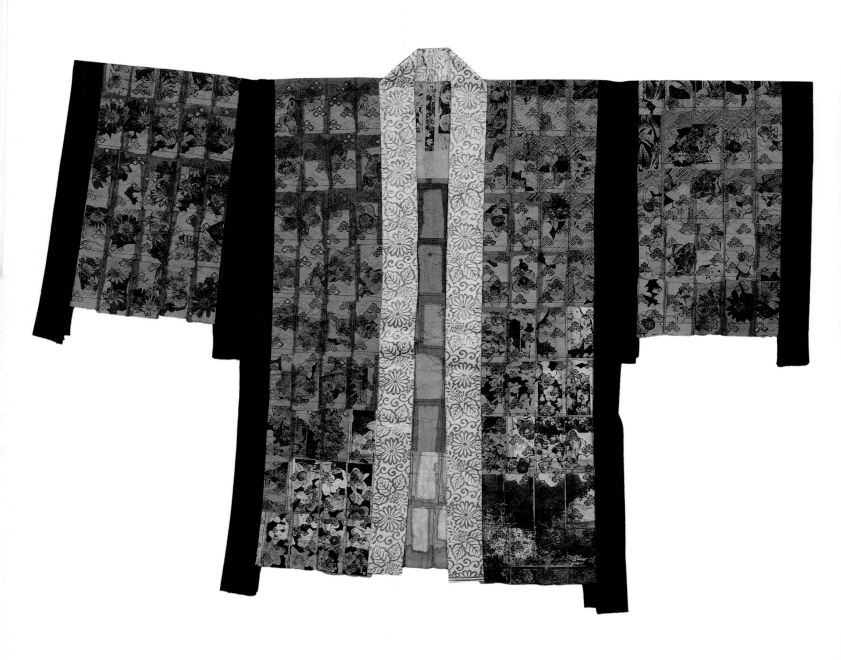

3·17 above

KATHERINE WESTPHAL American
(b. 1919)
Giverny II, 1983
Handmade paper, cotton, silk brocade, color
Xerox; dyed, stamped, patched

Westphal made her handmade paper wearable
by wrinkling and rolling it. Her *Giverny*
kimono series was inspired by a visit to
Monet's gardens; each one bears a copy of
a portrait of Monet or a photograph of one
of his paintings Xeroxed onto the paper.

3·18 opposite

KAISIK WONG American (1950–1990)
Orchid Dress, ca. 1976
Polyester jersey; airbrush-painted

This was a collaboration between Wong, who
conceived and made the dress, and artist and
musician Prairie Prince, who did the painting.
Wong often worked with synthetics instead of
silk, preferring them because no living being
was killed in their making.

3.19 above

NORMA MINKOWITZ American (b. 1937)
Formal Gardens Coat, 1985
Crocheted cotton, suede

Minkowitz's fine-grained work stands in
distinct contrast to the chunkier creations
of most crocheters, and made her one of the
few to continue using the technique in the
1980s when tastes favored smoother cloth
and sharper, more graphic imagery.

3.20 opposite

DINA KNAPP American (b. 1947)
Mother-of-Pearl Kimono, 1975
Wool, pearl buttons; crocheted, quilted,
appliquéd

This "kimono" derives from a Turkish, not
a Japanese, model. When she made this piece
Knapp was moving away from her focus
on crochet and chose to use it simply to
ornament a ground of commercial wool jersey,
gold on the back and dark red on the front.

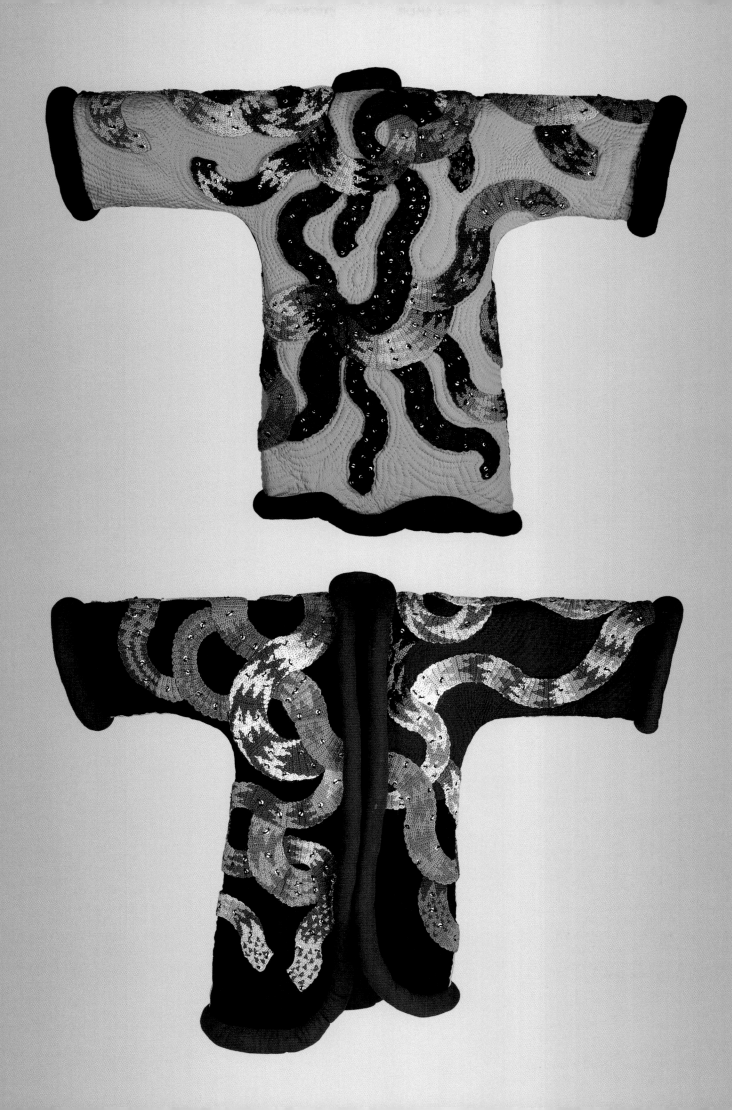

3.21 above

LINDA MENDELSON American (b. 1940)
Although I Called Another, Abra Came, 1998
Wool; loom-knitted, hand crocheted

Abra is the faithful companion and love first of
Aron, and then Caleb, Trask in Steinbeck's *East
of Eden*, a retelling of the story of Adam, Eve,
Cain, and Abel set in California's Salinas Valley.
The quotation comes from the eighteenth-
century satiric poem by Matthew Prior from
which Steinbeck's Abra got her name.

3.22 opposite

RISË NAGIN American (b. 1950)
Road Goliaths, 1985
Silk, cotton, acetate, polyester, acrylic paint;
pieced, appliquéd, and stained

The kimono's imagery and fractured picture
plane evokes a weighty truck rumbling by
on a mountain road. This was another of the
dozen examples of wearable art that toured
Europe in *Craft Today: U.S.A.*

3.23 above

DEBRA RAPOPORT American (b. 1945)
Hoop Hat with Beaded Flowers, 1993
Nineteenth-century cage crinoline, vintage
beaded flowers, millinery foliage, tinsel
cording, metallic fabric

This amazing picture hat is one of several
Rapoport made from hooped petticoats and
vintage millinery flowers combined with
contemporary materials. As an example of the
recycling of antiques in artwear it is unusual
in its use of Western and not Asian materials.

3.24 above right

REINA MIA BRILL American (b. 1971)
First Steps, 1999
Hand-knitted coated copper wire

Known for the endearing creatures she
creates as jewelry, Brill, whose work was
strongly influenced by Arline Fisch, was
drawn to knitted wire because of the scope
offered by its firmness and flexibility.

3.25 below right

ARLINE FISCH American (b. 1931)
Helen's Hat, 1985
Loom-knitted coated copper wire, silver
accents

Fisch pioneered the use of textile techniques
in jewelry, particularly the loom-knitting of
metal wire. The flexibility of her knitted
material allowed her to move beyond jewelry's
traditional small size and placement on the
body and create pieces like this one, which
push the boundary between jewelry and
artwear.

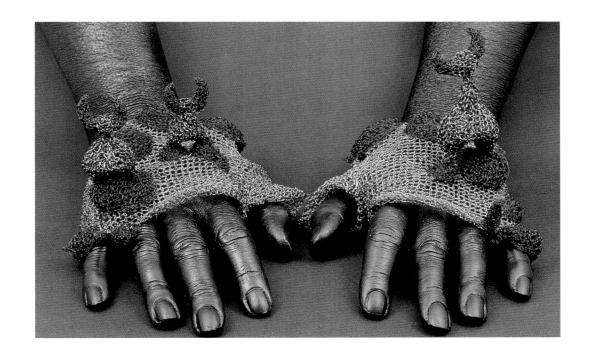

3.26 above

RANDALL DARWALL American (b. 1947)
Jacket, 1995
Silk; twill damask weave

In the 1990s Darwall, best known for
mesmerizing shawls and scarves that explore
the interaction of weave structure with color,
began making a limited number of garments
that were designed and woven in his studio
but constructed elsewhere.

3.27 above

DEBORAH VALOMA American (b. 1955)
Following Ariadne's Thread, 1992
Rayon, cotton; woven, dip-dyed

In the early 1990s Valoma moved from piecing and appliqué to weaving, forsaking bold colors for a quieter palette. The technique change brought greater depth to her characteristic, sharply graphic imagery but also helped her interest evolve away from garments. She now concentrates on woven vessels and hangings.

3.28 opposite

NINA VIVIAN HURYN American (b. 1952)
Water Lilies, Fish and Sleeping Skeleton, 1989
Painted silk satin; appliqué

To Huryn, skeletons represent humans in their
most elemental form. On this jacket, they seem
to occupy a dreamlike landscape, resting
sinuously underwater alongside the water lilies.

3.29 above left

K. LEE MANUEL American (1936–2003)
Dream of a Chinese Princess #1, 1990
Feathers, leather; painted, assembled

Manuel's feather collars exist in the gray area
between garment and jewelry. She discovered
her trademark feather medium accidentally,
learning by experimentation how to paint and
assemble them successfully.

3.30 above right

CANDACE KLING American (b.1948)
She Sells Sea Shells, 1988
Mixed media; molded, pleated, quilted, folded,
pressed, sewn

Kling imagined this satiny headdress as a fish
lying along the wearer's crown. However, it also
suggests the silhouette of the mohawk hairstyle
popular in Punk fashion since the 1970.

Dyeing is perhaps the most widely used
process in wearable art, whether alone as the
patterning method for cloth or in tandem
with structural processes like knitting, weaving,
crochet, felting, or piecing. Dyeing, and its
related techniques painting and printing, allows
an artist to concentrate on the all-important
features of surface design while working
with ready-made cloth. (A few involved in
production, like Marian Clayden, design
their own patterned textiles and have them
commercially woven to order, but this is
rare.) Dyeing offers artists endless scope for
experimentation with color, pattern, and
technique. In addition, a number of dyers
have described their attraction to the element
of surprise in resist-dyeing, finding that the
uncertainty over how, exactly, the resisted fabric
will take the dye or the way in which the dye
is removed when the fabric is discharged is
a tremendous spur to creativity and a constant
source of interest. Painting is the method most
directly related to the formal training many
artists have had. There are technical differences
to be mastered between painting on canvas

or paper and painting on silk, cotton, leather
or feathers, but the method of self-expression
evidently remains the same and the imagery
is often figurative (3.28, 3.29). Printing
encompasses a range of activities from stenciling
and screenprinting to photocopying, photo-
transfer, and letterpress, and imagery that ranges
from abstraction to text (4.3, 5.27). All three—
dyeing, painting, and printing—allow artists
to produce relatively large amounts of cloth
comparatively quickly. The dyer Carter Smith
recently estimated that over his thirty-five-year
career he has dyed close to 200,000 yards of
fabric[9]; and, though few others have aspired to
such quantity, speedier methods are undoubtedly
a boon, especially to those engaged in production.

Fabric manipulation techniques like folding,
pleating, tucking, twisting, and ruching often
appear in tandem with dyeing since, of course,
many of these techniques are part of resist-
dyeing processes. The artist has the option of
ironing them out, or retaining them as part
of the texture and pattern of the dyed fabric,
as Ana Lisa Hedstrom did to great effect in
Samurai Vest (1980), *Moiré Vest* (1981), and

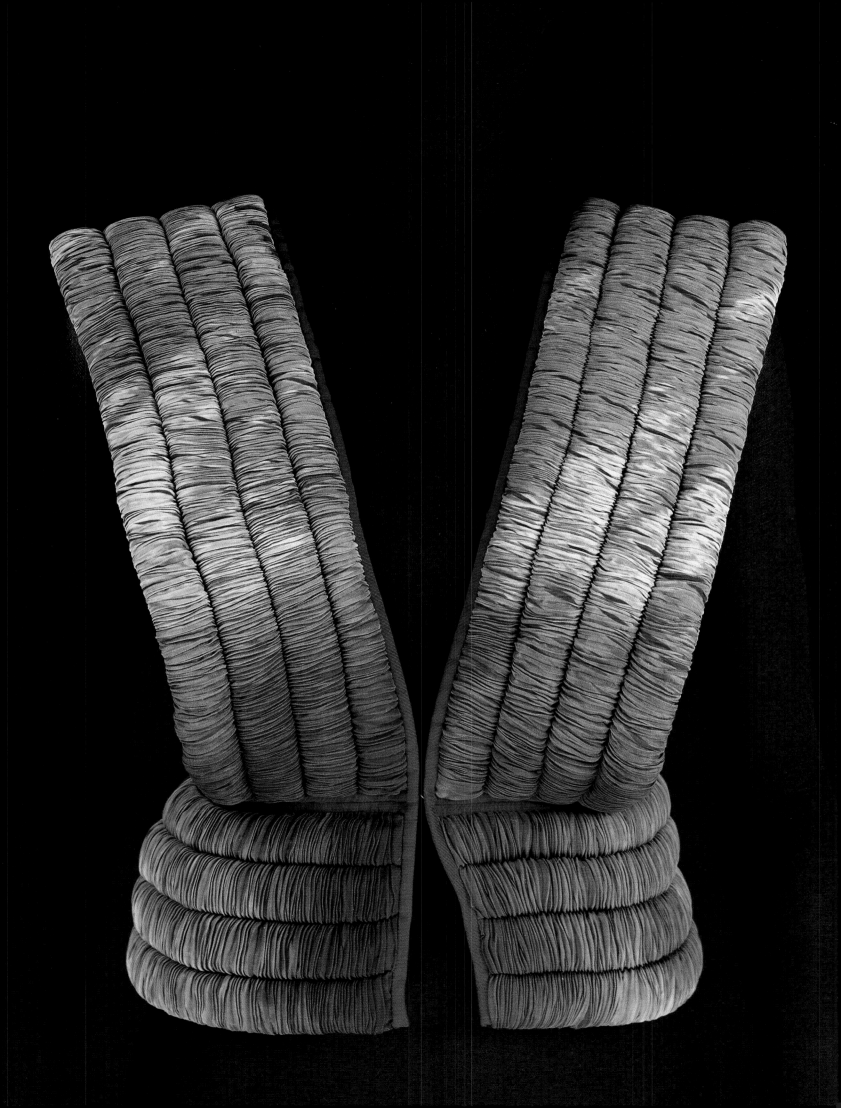

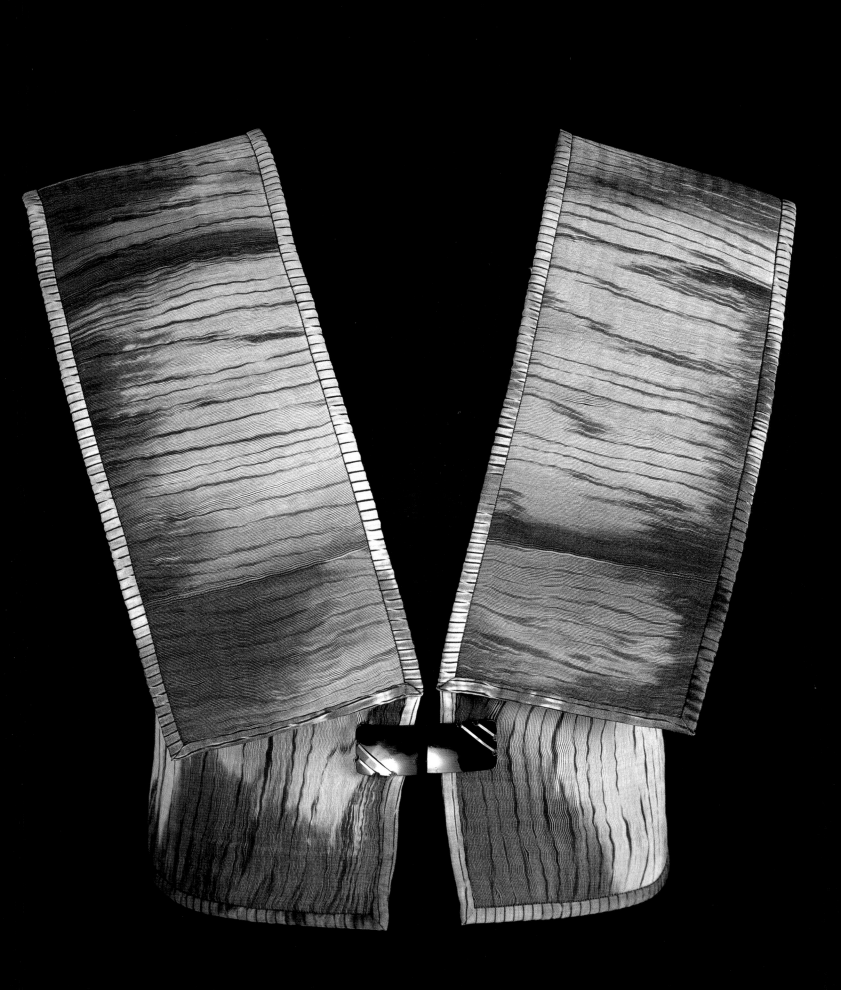

ANA LISA HEDSTROM American (b. 1943)
Samurai Vest and *Moiré Vest*, 1979–82
Shibori-dyed silk

These slender vests recall aspects of Japanese armor. Hedstrom chose to incorporate the pleats and ruching used in the dyeing process into the design of both vests.

3.33 below left

CAROL LEE SHANKS American (b. 1957)
Scarification Fairy (skirt, wrap, and vest), 2001
Gunma silk; pieced, bundle-resisted, stitch-resisted, scoured

Shanks likens silk to skin, and the creases and pleats made by the resist process to decorative scarification. Her airy silk came from Yoshiko Wada's Project Metamorphosis, which offered special fabric woven in Japan's Gunma Prefecture to selected artists and designers, hoping to encourage continued silk production there.

3.34 below right

BEN COMPTON American (1938–1986) and MARIAN CLAYDEN working in U.S. (b. U.K., 1937)
Nocturnal Moth, 1974
Super organza, steel corset stays, nylon "horsehair" braid, silk veiling, cotton lace, elasticized harness; dyed, clamped, discharged, dipped, burned, cut, pieced, stitched

Compton, a New York–based theatrical costume and fashion designer, and Clayden, a California dyer, collaborated long-distance on this piece, which was made for the 1974 *Bodywear* exhibition at the Oakland Museum of California.

3.35 opposite

NANCY CHAPPELL American (b. 1938)
Dragon Dress, 1995
Silk, satin, and silk and metal organza, couched gold thread embroidery, tassels

Many of Chappell's wearable art pieces from the 1980s and 90s recycle vintage Asian textiles. This evening dress was made from a fragment of an antique Chinese dragon robe augmented with new satin, organza, and trim.

Fan Vest (1983) (1.8, 3.31, 3.32), and as the Canadian-born artist Genevieve Dion often does in her silk and velvet clothes and accessories (3.37). Pleating is probably the most common of the manipulation techniques, employed by artists in silk, velvet, and polyester garments both as a by-product of dyeing and as a fabric manipulation technique on its own; it can be used to create a surprisingly broad range of visual and textural effects. Pleating is also a time-honored way of fitting fabric to the body, and pleated garments are also often more body-conscious than some other forms of wearable art, although artists such as the headdress-maker Candace Kling also use pleating and other forms of fabric manipulation to alter rather than reveal the body (3.30).

Virtually all the processes detailed above may be used in collage or assemblage, which, as Miriam Schapiro has pointed out, are twentieth-century art-world terms for long-used craft techniques associated with women's work, like piecing and appliqué. Collage, loosely defined

as pictures assembled from assorted materials,[10] has a broad range of applications in artwear in creating pattern, color, and texture as well as pictures. Collage encompasses handmade textiles created from commercially made materials or recycled ones (3.35); artists also use it to add dimension to textiles they have already processed. Appliqué is widespread, piecing slightly less so, and most artists combine them with a multitude of other processes.

Meanings

In her preface to Julie Schafler Dale's *Art to Wear*, Jean Druesedow comments that the primary difference between artwear and other forms of costume design is the former's addition of subject matter.[11] It is tempting to take this to mean that artwear is usually *about* something extrinsic to the clothing itself. But that is not always the case. There is wearable art, much of it very good, that, rather like Minimalist art, focuses primarily on the garment's formal

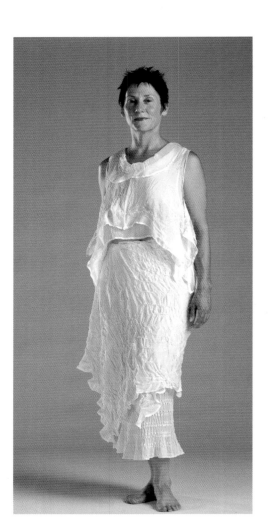

3.36 above

JANET LIPKIN American (b. 1948)
Flamingo, 1982
Loom-knitted, hand-dyed wool

Birds are recurring motifs in Lipkin's work.

aesthetic properties: the artist's sense of beauty, interest in pattern, passion for color, eye for composition (3.33). Carol Lee Shanks's airy, layered ensembles, for example, or Jacquelyn Roesch-Sanchez's beautiful shaded meditations on color come alive when they are worn, and the act of wearing imbues them with all the complex covert and overt meanings that clothing has in Western culture, but they are not necessarily in and of themselves full of meaning about something else. As is discussed further in Chapter 5, the focus on an external subject is one of the ways dress gets itself taken seriously in art and academia, and there is a related tendency to regard purely aesthetic works as less important, although they are not. Nonetheless, there are many examples of artwear that do have an analyzable subject or outlook and it is possible to identify a few major themes.

Probably the single most common theme is nature, or the natural world—not surprising considering the pervasive interest in the environment over the past generation and the prominence of nature imagery in both Japanese art and in many of wearable art's antecedent movements. Work after work references nature, from vaguely organic forms to increasingly sophisticated plant and marine life, insects, reptiles, and birds, sometimes rendered impressionistically through color and materials, as in Ben Compton and Marian Clayden's *Nocturnal Moth* (1974) (3.34), or anthropomorphically, as in Susanna Lewis's *Moth Cape* (1979), a heavy, loom-knitted and crocheted cape in the shape of a moth, which, when worn, appears to be enveloping the wearer in its wings.[12] Landscape has proven to be especially popular, particularly as imagery on coats. Artists may be portraying or symbolically evoking a particular place, such as Joan Steiner's ode to her family kitchen (3.39) and Jean Williams Cacicedo's to Wyoming, or referencing a particular time of year or day, as does the hot marshland sunset of Judith Content's *Sweltering Sky* (1992) (1.9). Landscapes allow the wearer to express symbolic unity with his or her real or imagined surroundings, and, given their complexity of imagery, they are also often *tours-de-force* of technique.

Language appears in a wide variety of ways in wearable art (3.46). Linda Mendelson's major work relies on varying degrees of verbiage, from a few words to long lines of text that themselves become the piece's imagery (3.40). Text might appear as a mantra or reminder, as it does in Gaza Bowen's *K. Lee, You're On Your Own* (1983) (3.45), or hint at underlying social and semantic meanings, as in Charlotte Kruk n' Kempken's *Peach Nectar* (2003) (3.43). Louise Todd Cope's *Poetry Shirt* (1978) (3.38) was conceived as a publication, a book of seventeen poems by Donald J. Willcox to be worn.[13] Another wearable book, albeit one that includes little text, is Frances Butler's *New Dryads Dress* (1979) (3.44), a letterpress-printed organdy pinafore with pockets to hold the plates of a portfolio of printed text and images of people dressed "to look good."[14] Language in the Surrealist sense of visual puns is also present in artwear, both incorporated into objects themselves and worked into their titles. Jean Williams Cacicedo's *Rain Coat* (2001) is a good example of both: the coat's title is punched into its hem below a torrent of punched raindrops that would render it useless against the real thing (3.47).

Pop Art paved the way for the use of everyday life and popular culture as themes, also often incorporating language like song lyrics as well as familiar imagery that has been appropriated and recontextualized. Susan Summa's taxi-bedecked *Life's More Fun When You Travel in a Checker* (1995) (3.41) portrays a familiar image from day-to-day life. So does Yoshiko Wada's ikat-dyed *Coca-Cola Kimono* (1975) (3.48), which uses Coke's familiar logo to satirize traditional Japanese kimono patterning tradition while commenting backhandedly on the successful cultural and economic exchange between America and Japan. Dina Knapp's coat *See It Like a Native* (1982) (3.2) suggests some of the darker sides of American life, setting off Florida's famous pink flamingos with a disturbing image-and-object collage of guns, war planes, dolls, black faces, and blood.

The theme of transformation runs throughout artwear. Of course, the act of dressing transforms our naked, private selves into our clothed, public selves; in that sense, transformation is the universal subject of clothing. But the subject matter incorporated into wearable art brings transformation to a more conscious, theatrical level, and this may be why it is important to so many artists to see their work on the body. By donning a piece, the wearer can at will become a butterfly, a tulip, a flamingo, or a lizard (3.36); be languishing in the desert, lost in a dense oak forest, in the middle of a private rainstorm, or snug in the family kitchen (3.42). He or she can put on a headdress and become a crustacean (or a punk sporting a mohawk, depending on your point of view), a participant in a Venetian masquerade, or the egg warmed and sheltered by a nesting bird (3.49, 3.50). The wearer carries the artist's vision, which then melds with the wearer's as he or she moves within each piece and brings it to life in real space and time. Artwear just may be the ultimate art of communal dressing up.

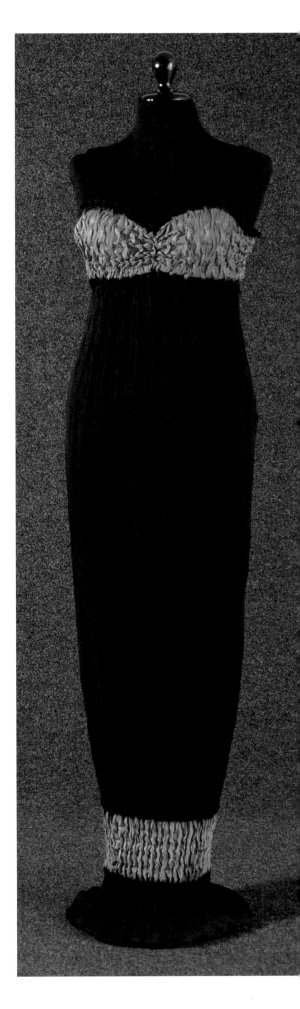

3.37 right

GENEVIEVE DION working in U.S. (b. Canada, 1963)
Mermaid Dress, 1999
Gunma silk; shibori scoured and dyed

Dion often uses the crumpling and pleating of the shibori dyeing process to fit her garments to the body.

3.38 above

LOUISE TODD COPE American (b. 1930)
Created in collaboration with the Fabric
Workshop and Museum, Philadelphia
Poetry Shirt, 1978
Silkscreen on linen

This wearable "book" of poetry was conceived
as an alternative to a traditional publication.

3.39 opposite

JOAN STEINER American
Kitchen Vest, 1977
Velvet, cotton, rayon, satin, found objects;
pieced, collaged

Based on the kitchen in Steiner's family home,
this vest nostalgically evokes an American
postwar suburban kitchen, with its gleaming
appliances, rug-strewn linoleum floor, and
lace-trimmed curtains. The vest literally puts
a woman *in* the kitchen, but it is one that the
wearer can take with her out into the world.

3.40 left

LINDA MENDELSON American (b. 1940)
I Made My Song a Coat, 1976
Loom-knitted wool

Text and music references are Mendelson
trademarks. This coat's title, which is knitted
across its shoulders, is the first line of William
Butler Yeats's 1916 poem *A Coat*:

> I made my song a coat
> Covered with embroideries
> Out of old mythologies
> From heel to throat;
> But the fools caught it,
> Wore it in the world's eyes
> As though they'd wrought it.
> Song, let them take it
> For there's more enterprise
> In walking naked.

3.41 above

SUSAN SUMMA American (b. 1948)
Life's More Fun When You Travel in a Checker,
1995
Loom-knitted wool

The punning title of Summa's chieftain
cloak refers both to its checkerboard pattern
and the familiar Checker cabs that race
around its hem.

3.42 opposite

NICKI HITZ EDSON American (b. 1941)
Seascape Kimono, 1987
Loom-knitted wool

Edson's coats often depict nature; the colors
of this one evoke rocky red hills rising above
a deep blue, foam-flecked sea.

3.43 right

CHARLOTTE KRUK N' KEMPKEN
American (b. 1971)
Peach Nectar, 2002
Mixed media

Kruk n' Kempken's "wearable sculptures"
made of recycled food and candy packaging
comment on American throwaway society
and views of women. This punning "fruit
cocktail" dress is made of unused peach
nectar labels. The ruffle at the center back
of her skirt implies that the wearer's sweetness
is artificial—those labels are stamped "pack
in saccharin."

3.44 left

FRANCES BUTLER American (b. 1940)
New Dryads Dress, 1979
Organdy, paper; letterpress-printed,
hand-colored

Butler's many-pocketed pinafore holds
miniature versions of a large portfolio
of street fashions and texts. She saw the
miniatures as a moving index to the
portfolio, suggesting the process of looking at clothing
and emphasizing the fluidity of cloth,
a favorite theme. The front plate is a self-
portrait of Butler wearing one of her own
fabric prints.

3.45 below left

GAZA BOWEN American (1944–2005)
K. Lee, You're On Your Own, 1983
Kidskin, lizard, leather, wine corks, rubber

Made as a gift for the artist K. Lee Manuel
to commemorate her divorce, her youngest
child's college graduation, and her move
to San Francisco, these shoes sport familiar
San Francisco landmarks like the Golden
Gate Bridge.

3.46 opposite

JO ELLEN TRILLING American
Western Fringed Jacket, 1989
Cotton and found objects; drawing and
assemblage

The language on this jacket is as enigmatic
as the rest of the imagery. Words that connote
movement and direction and that begin
with the letters *a* or *b*—about, above, across,
after, before, behind, beyond, beside, between,
beneath—tumble across the yoke, above
a drawing of the God of Love asleep.

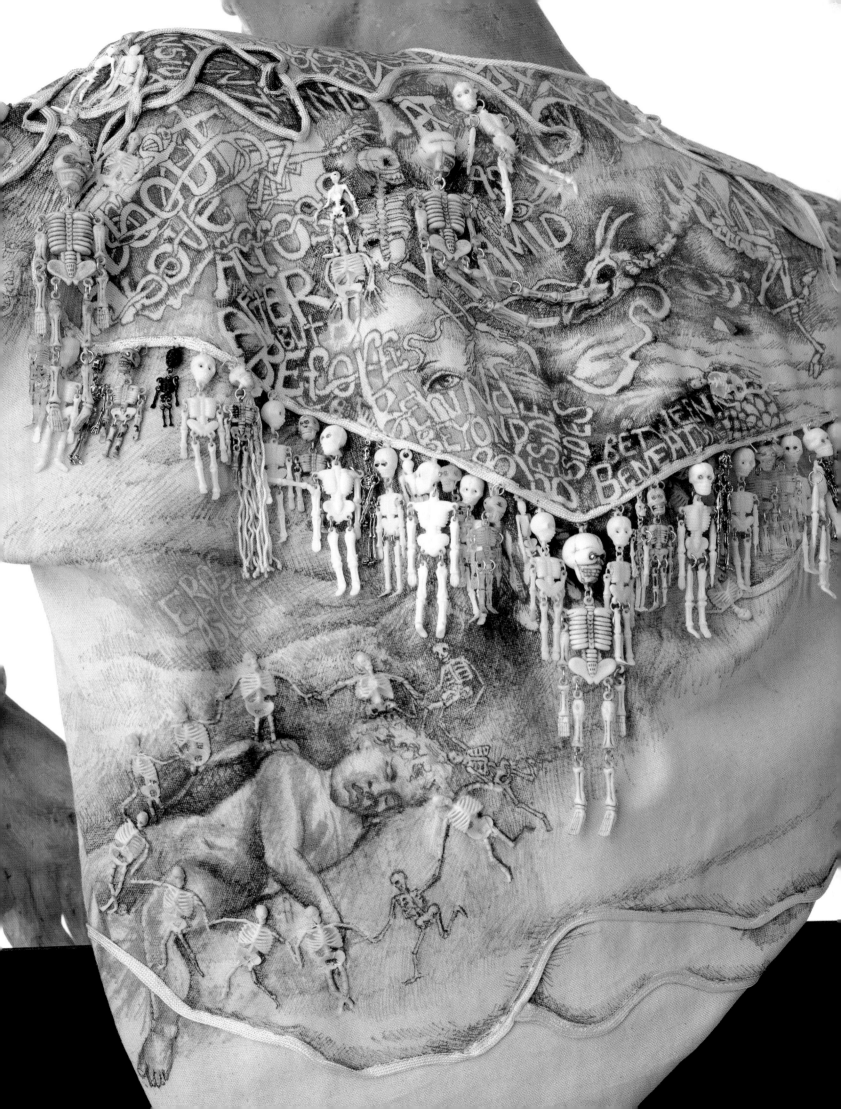

3.47 above

JEAN WILLIAMS CACICEDO
American (b. 1948)
Rain Coat: San Francisco Bay, 1999
Wool knit; fulled, dyed, slashed, pieced

Cacicedo often depicts specific, personally significant places in her coats, and in this commissioned work she also included elements that are meaningful to the coat's owner. It features views of Marin County, the owner's home, and San Francisco from Berkeley, where the artist lives, and the bridges that connect the three. The landmark buildings along the coat's bottom are three that the owner's husband, a structural engineer, worked to seismically retrofit.

3.48 opposite

YOSHIKO WADA working in U.S.
(b. Japan, 1945)
Coca-Cola Kimono, 1975
Linen; weft-ikat

Ikat is a wrap-resist process in which a pattern is dyed onto bundles of yarn before it is woven into cloth. The motifs on the finished cloth have characteristically blurred edges. Complex motifs like the Coca-Cola logo are created through a variation known as *e-gasuri,* or "picture ikat."

3.49 following spread, left

KENNETH D. KING American (b. 1958)
Lucifer's Handmaiden, 1993
Taffeta, velvet, feathers, and beads

King's befeathered hat is in the form of a mask, ready to be pulled down over its wearer's eyes should she need to conceal her identity.

3.50 following spread, right

NORMA MINKOWITZ American (b. 1937)
Sit on It, 1980; *Headdress II,* 1975
Cotton, wool; crocheted, knitted, stuffed, stiffened, painted

The nesting bird recalls non-Western ceremonial hats that identify the wearer with the animal perched atop his or her head. The other headdress bristles with flat, round, and tentacled forms that suggest plant or clinging marine life.

4   Artwear Outside the U.S.A.

Wearable art as an identifiable subset of the craft revival movement developed first in the United States, and its main story has been played out there; but it is not solely an American phenomenon. To give a comprehensive description and analysis of artwear outside the United States is beyond the scope of the book, but this chapter will summarize the development of the genre in Britain and Europe, Australia, New Zealand, Korea, and Japan. There are, however, some key differences. Although artwear outside the United States developed out of a similar cultural ferment in the 1970s, it seems more firmly rooted in its craft origins, less concerned with charting an identity separate from fashion and the clothing industry, and less determined to achieve acceptance by the art world on its own terms. The use of ethnic, nonfashion garment forms is not nearly as prevalent, and textile artists often make artwear as only one part of a more general career that includes wall hangings or other flat textiles. There are also many small design houses using handmade textiles that identify themselves more with the fashion than with the art or craft worlds. There are numerous traveling exhibitions, conferences, networks, and in some cases galleries, but artwear has not been highlighted in the same way as it has in the United States. In Europe in particular, wearable art seems less likely to be identified, or encouraged, as an endeavor separate from either fiber art or fashion.

Just as American artists drew from non-Western cultures, outreach from the United States—from artists traveling for teaching, exhibitions, and meetings, and from American artists residing abroad—most likely had an influence on artwear in Europe and Asia. In 1980, for instance, the World Crafts Council board invited artist Katherine Westphal to present programs on American wearable art at its meeting in Vienna that year (3.3). Westphal invited three colleagues from the University of California at Davis to join her—Debra Rapoport, Jo Ann Stabb, and Dolph Gotelli—and together the four saturated Vienna with a comprehensive mix of artwear workshops, lectures, and dress-up events.[1] Touring exhibitions from the American Craft Museum also had influence. *Art to Wear: New Handmade Clothing*, an exhibition of forty-seven garments by twenty-four artists, began a tour of Asia in 1984 and has been credited with sparking the interest in wearable art among Korean fiber artists, museums, and universities that led to the genre becoming established there.[2] *Craft Today: U.S.A.*, a traveling version of the American Craft Museum's *Craft Today: The Poetry of the Physical*, visited a dozen countries in Western and Eastern Europe, Scandinavia, and Central Asia, from 1989 to 1993. The exhibition included only fourteen works of wearable art (excluding jewelry), but set them within the wider context of American studio craft at the end of the 1980s.

The European Spectrum

The terms *art to wear* and *wearable art* seem never to have caught on in Britain, which suggests less of a focus on acceptance by the art world—or perhaps just different methods of trying to achieve it. It may be significant that, in contrast to the American mix-and-match educational system where exploration and boundary-crossing are encouraged by the structure of the curriculum, the various

disciplines are more firmly segregated in Britain, and fine art and craft thus have separate training programs with comparatively little overlap. Britons who make wearables often come through formal textile training programs and may also produce fiber art, in contrast to Americans who tend to remain firmly associated with garments and who often come to artwear through nontextile arts disciplines. It has been suggested that, as a result of their different forms of training, the Britons are technically more accomplished, while the Americans are more freely creative,[3] but there are some indications that this distinction was blurring in the 1990s. Perhaps even more important, fine arts and crafts have had separate sources of government funding and support, which doubtless encouraged artists to make a strong identification with one or the other.[4]

Whatever the reasons, the result is that the concept of art clothing in Britain embraces work that may be more craft-oriented, more fashionable, or more conceptual than that of its American cousins. And there is infrastructure to support all three varieties. Clothes made from finely crafted handmade textiles may be shown in exhibitions, craft fairs, and numerous craft galleries across the country. There is regular coverage in *Crafts* magazine, and government support in the form of the British Crafts Council, which offers artists' grants, mounts exhibitions, and maintains galleries, shops, archives, and a collection. There are also numerous training programs in weaving and a variety of surface design techniques, some within prestigious institutions like the Royal College of Art in London. Many of the hundreds of talented craftspeople with this training have gone into the kind of small- and medium-scale limited

production that has characterized much American artwear, emphasizing fine craftsmanship in garments that are within the scope of current fashion while not necessarily seeking to be ultrafashionable. Support comes from various guilds and a large and enthusiastic population of amateurs, enabling some of those craftspeople to build influential and lucrative businesses. The Welsh knitter Sasha Kagan, for example, for twenty-five years has been designing floral sweaters that are hand-knitted to order by her studio team, but she has developed a larger business based on instructional books and classes, and dozens of different knitting kits. The transplanted American Kaffe Fassett, originally a painter, parlayed his taste for wild colors first into high-end, one-of-a-kind knitwear and design for commercial production in the 1960s and 70s, before creating a do-it-yourself empire of books, lectures, and television shows that encompasses knitwear and textiles, patchwork and needlepoint, and that, like Kagan's business, serves a multinational audience.

While British artists talk about their desire to make textiles and clothing free from the constraints of the fashion world, they usually seem quite willing to use fashionable forms, and to embrace the world of fashion in various ways.[5] One example is shoemaker Thea Cadabra, who made finely crafted one-of-a-kind and very-limited-edition shoes in the late 1970s and 80s that were at once full of whimsy, popular culture references, and social commentary, and also eminently wearable (4.4, 4.5). Another is milliner Deirdre Hawken, who makes tiny, surreal, faux-food-trimmed hats that sport slices of melon, plates of salad, or bunches of chili peppers. A third is the British group the New RenaisCAnce, essentially a small, exclusive fashion house with

a strong crafts base. It was founded in 1990 by four graduates of the Royal College of Art—fashion designer Harvey Bertram-Brown, textile designer and embroiderer Carolyn Corben, jeweler Sophie Harley, and spectacle-frame designer Felicity Jury Cramp. *Crafts* magazine cited their "Arts & Crafts approach" and likened them to Morris & Co., though more for their high prices than for their methodology.[6] Their early work was extravagantly decorative and sometimes edgy; they made one-of-a-kind and limited-edition fashionable clothes from hand-painted, printed, and embroidered textiles and from found objects, with jewelry and spectacles to match (4.1). Their clothes were carried by purveyors of craft and high fashion such as Liberty's, Harvey Nichols, and Browns in London, and Henri Bendel in New York, and appeared in avant-garde fashion shows like "The Pleasure Revenge Show" at Hyper Hall in Denmark in 1996. They also appeared, however, on the art gallery circuit, showing at the London gallery Fouts and Fowler, in the Saatchi and Saatchi exhibition at the Royal Festival Hall, and at the Parco Gallery in Tokyo, all in 1991.[7]

Fashion has formed the basis for the work of artists like Helen Storey, who first emerged in the late 1980s as an innovative and controversial fashion designer. In the mid-1990s Storey forsook commercial fashion and teamed up with her sister Kate, a developmental biologist, to design an ambitious wearable art series entitled *Primitive Streak*. Funded initially by a grant from the Wellcome Trust's Sciart project, which commissions artworks that aim to make science more accessible to ordinary people, *Primitive Streak* is a series of twenty-seven dresses that represent ten separate stages in the first thousand hours of human life (4.6). They are a deft fusion of fashion and science with craft and art. Storey designed but did not make the dresses, relying instead on a host of craftspeople, workers in the fashion industry, and staff and students at the London College of Fashion. The dresses themselves uniquely combine traditional materials and crafts processes like silk and embroidery with cutting-edge materials and technologies like resins, plastics, and fiber optics.

A similar, though less technologically extreme, fusion is found in Susie Freeman's work for the *Pharmacopoeia* project, created in collaboration with doctor Liz Lee and video artist David Critchley, and also funded by the Wellcome Trust's Sciart. *Pharmacopoeia*, which began

in 1998, is a series of artworks that explores the impact of prescription drugs on daily life. Freeman's contributions are flat textiles and fashionably styled garments made of her trademark translucent nylon monofilament fabric loom-knitted with small pockets, which she uses to hold and display found objects or artifacts from daily life. For each *Pharmacopoeia* piece, Freeman filled the pockets with items that have medical significance; one evening dress is decorated with twenty-six years' worth of brightly colored birth-control pills (4.2), and another, a maternity dress, bristles with 840 cigarette butts, the number that would result from smoking a pack a week for nine months.[8]

In the 1980s, especially, jewelry artists rethinking the field's parameters, not just in Britain but in the Netherlands and Australia, were also making what were essentially clothing accessories—collars, cuffs, ruffs, veils, hats —and abandoning precious materials in favor of natural and synthetic textiles like paper, fur, rubber, wood, and nonprecious metals. Caroline Broadhead, whose work will be discussed at greater length in Chapter 5, is probably the best known of the Britons in this category; others include Julia Mannheim, and Susanna Heron, who was making dyed nylon ruffs and sculptural fur, felt, and metal hats (4.8, 4.9) at the same time that Broadhead was making expandable cuffs, sleeves, and shirts from cotton, silk, and stretchy woven nylon (4.7). Significantly, in the introduction to the exhibition catalogue *Crosscurrents*, Heron sounds some of the same themes familiar from artwear in the United States, particularly in her description of a felt and metal hat, which, when not worn, is intended to hang on the wall.[10]

British jewelers, Broadhead in particular, were influential in bringing their ideas to the Netherlands in the late 1970s, and by the early 80s similar concerns and boundary-dissolving pieces could be found, for instance, in painted cotton collars by Claudie Berbée and Joke Brakman, and wood and textile hats and collars by Lam de Wolf (4.13). Much of the work is sculptural, more involved with form than surface and reliant on a specific position on the body. It greatly increased the primacy of jewelry—de Wolf noted that her "wearable objects" were so dominant when worn that great care had to be taken in choosing the clothing that went with them rather than the other way

4.6 above

HELEN STOREY British (b. 1959)
Spinal Column Dress, 1997, from the
Primitive Streak Collection
Printed silk, silver foil, and fiber optics

Primitive Streak, twenty-seven dresses exploring the ten key events in the first 1,000 hours of human life, fuses art with science. The pattern on this dress is based on a rat's DNA sequence, and the female spine, cast in silver-foil-plated resin, is threaded with 8,000 fiber-optic endings that represent the body's nerve processes.

4.7 left

CAROLINE BROADHEAD British
(b. 1950)
Sleeve, 1981
Nylon monofilament; dyed and woven

Pieces like this sleeve, made from non-precious materials and completely flexible in form, mark the early stages of Broadhead's transition from jewelry to garments.

4.8 above right

SUSANNA HERON British (b. 1949)
Wearable, 1982
Cotton jersey, steel; knotted

Heron began to call her functional work "Wearable" rather than jewelry in the early 1980s, suggesting its broader scope. This hat is worn as if it had just been pushed off the head; it is about the space around the neck and shoulders and the relationship of the circle form to the body.

4.9 below right

SUSANNA HERON British (b. 1949)
Ruff, 1983
Nylon dyed with five different blacks

The ruff, originally fashionable in the sixteenth and seventeenth centuries, reappears in fashion periodically, usually smaller and more necklacelike. It is also worn by clowns. Heron's oversized version, worn here by a dancer, connotes both garment and performance costume, and was intended to be exotic and glamorous.

4.10 – 4.12 following page

Felt—warm, light, and skinlike—is currently very popular as a medium for artwear. Its applications range from German artist Katharina Thomas's enveloping wedding ensemble (1987), to headgear like Jeannette Sendler's triballike hat (1999), to the Swiss artist Käthi Hoppler-Dinkel's *Schritt-für-Schritt-Stiefel* (2000), a pair of charming valasian and merino wool felt boots that look ready to lift their wearer into the air.

4.13 opposite

LAM DE WOLF Dutch (b. 1949)
Headdress, 1984
Textile, wood, paint

De Wolf's collars, body pieces, and head-dresses are intended to make their wearers highly conscious of the way they stand and move, and to dominate, not accessorize, an ensemble. De Wolf has commented of this body of work that, while it functions perfectly well as sculpture, it takes on an added dimension when worn.

around[10]—and gave the jeweler a far more active and direct influence over the wearer's consciousness of her body.

This same preoccupation with form rather than surface design characterizes the work of other Dutch artists, particularly milliners like Mirjam Nuver, who works in straw, and Edith Verhoeven, who works in felt. Maria Blaisse's work deals with both larger and smaller garments that transform the appearance and movement of the body through the use of form, color, and unlikely materials, such as industrial rubber, thermoplastics, and foam, and processes like vacuum molding. Blaisse was trained in textile design, and her first garment was the Flexicap, made from an inner tube and picked up by Issey Miyake for his 1988 collection. Much of her subsequent work is highly and theatrically sculptural, and rather cold in a way that makes it less likely to work on the runway; and indeed, though wearable, it is not intended for street-wear. Instead, as curator Aaron Betsky has noted, Blaisse has been intent on exploring the inherent geometric order within each stuff she works with and then exploiting it to transform the body into something that is familiar but that at the same time we don't quite recognize.[11] In order for its transformative effects and its look in motion to be appreciated, she usually shows it on dancers in performance.

For every artist like Blaisse or the Briton Robin Giddings, whose work explores new materials and techniques (4.21), there is an artist like Käthi Hoppler-Dinkel working in felt, thought to be the oldest textile technique. The revival in feltmaking was sparked by the work of

the Briton Mary Burkett in the 1960s and 70s, and interest in it has risen steadily ever since, particularly among artists in Germany, the Netherlands, Eastern Europe, and Scandinavia (4.10).[12] A number of felters' organizations have sprung up in various countries in Europe, as well as in North America, Australia, and New Zealand, and there is also an International Feltmakers' Association that offers opportunities for artists from all over the world to exhibit their work and to network with and learn from each other (4.15).

At the moment, felt is decidedly "in" as a material for both wearables and nonwearables. Felt has always been used in hatmaking, but artists are stretching its applications further afield, to dresses, coats, handbags, suits, and to installation pieces (4.14). Hoppler-Dinkel makes "foot envelopes," delightful, whimsical boots with wide, airy, multicolored, and multilayered tops that not only mold to the foot as they are worn but look as if they are about to lift the wearer into the air (4.12). The works of Jeannette Sendler, a German artist working in Britain, range from sculptural, triballike hats to a series of ghostly white costumes made for a performance work staged in a cemetery (4.11).[13] Felt requires time and a particular kind of rhythmic physical effort to make,[14] and artists often express a profound spiritual connection to it. Many reference felt's skinlike properties, which can trigger visceral reactions in both maker and viewer. In addition, as with resist-dyeing, there is an element of surprise in the felting process that many artists find very engaging.

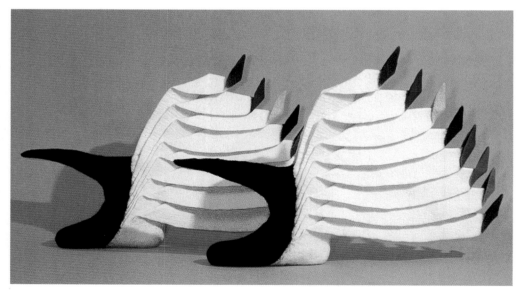

Felt is extremely tactile, but much of the patterning found in felt currently is abstract and irregular (4.32). European artists interested primarily in more representational or smoother surfaces tend to gravitate to other methods of figuring cloth, relying on both traditional handcraft methods and, increasingly since the late 1980s, on exploring and exploiting the kinds of high-tech and industrial materials and processes that artists like Blaisse and Storey have used. Shibori has been the focus of much of that work, since it lends itself readily to industrial processes while maintaining its status as traditional craft, and it has been promoted through the activities of the World Shibori Network, which was set up in 1992 as an outgrowth of the first International Shibori Symposium in Nagoya that year. There is now an active group of shibori dyers in Scandinavia and elsewhere in Europe, some of whom make wearable art.[15] Shibori was, of course, seen in wearable art in Europe prior to 1992. In the late 1980s, Jane Harris, in Scotland at the time, was producing beautiful, fluid, and extremely labor-intensive shibori-dyed silk and synthetic garments. She has subsequently used her experience with shibori and knowledge of textiles as the basis for tremendously innovative work in virtual reality (4.16). The Swiss artist Mascha Mioni came to shibori from an earlier

incarnation as a painter of representational works in oil on canvas and on textiles. An encounter with Amish quilts on a tour of the United States in the early 1980s led her to shift her artistic focus to abstract and geometric forms animated by color, and in the late 1980s she began to create wearable art. Mioni founded a group called the Art to Wear Team in 1989, which has mounted periodic exhibitions in Switzerland, Germany, and the United States, and has published two books on the subject. She is dedicated to helping it find legitimacy as an art form in much the same way as American artists have been.[16] Mioni's garments, like those of Blaisse and her Australian counterpart Patricia Black, are essentially kinetic sculptures that are animated by the body; despite her expressed desire to put artwear on people's backs these pieces are, by and large, not streetwear.

Shibori has found itself a home in a variety of countries, while in Europe silk painting seems to have become associated primarily with Germany. Silk painters found a strong champion in Rudolf Smend of Galerie Smend in Cologne. Galerie Smend opened in 1973 selling Indonesian batik; within a decade Smend was showing artwear and art textiles alongside the batik. Although the gallery is known for painted silks, it has also shown wearable art and contemporary textiles patterned by other, mainly resist-dyeing,

4.14 previous spread, left

THOMAS HORST American (b. 1971)
Aflame, 2002
Wool; felted

Horst, an emerging artist, has designed *Aflame* to conform to a fashionable evening dress silhouette and rendered it in felt, currently a very popular material for artwear.

4.15 previous spread, right

JORIE JOHNSON working in Japan (b. U.S., 1954)
Confetti Wedding Cocoon, 2004
Wool, flock-printed silk organza, mohair, polyester novelty yarns; felted, machine-stitched

Johnson has created a layered figured felt that attenuates to a lacelike texture at the cuffs in keeping with the lace that often adorns traditional Western wedding dress.

4.16 below

JANE HARRIS British (b. 1965)
Kinetic Series, 1991–94
Silk and synthetic; shibori-constructed and dyed

In the *Kinetic Series*, Harris examined the interaction between clothes and the moving body using lightweight textiles that, when lit, allowed the body beneath the cloth to appear like a kinetic X-ray. Harris now explores similar ideas using computer animation, basing her digital garments on her understanding of the real thing.

4.17 right

MASCHA MIONI Swiss (b. 1941)
MohnTag (Poppy Day), 1999
Silk; shibori-dyed

Mioni's dramatic artwear, shown here
with one of her paintings, layers
swaths of bold color and fabric over
the armature provided by the body
beneath. Her garments are more like
sculptures set in motion by the wearer
than like streetwear, and she often
presents them in performance.

methods like shibori and ikat.[17] Smend has organized a number of artwear shows at the gallery and, beginning in 1983, he published an impressive series of five biennial catalogues that highlighted both artwear and flat textiles made primarily from painted silk. The gallery has also functioned as a learning center by holding workshops on various painting and dyeing techniques taught by a broad spectrum of artists and craftspeople. The German style of wearable art—as gleaned from Galerie Smend's catalogues—is a blend of nonfashion and fashion. The expected kimonos and caftans (4.18) are accompanied by works that feature flowing, brilliantly colored silk draperies (4.20), and a substantial number of fitted garments in fashionable shapes that plainly are aimed at a fashion audience (4.19). The motifs themselves may be either abstract or representational; the watercolorlike properties of the medium lend themselves equally to subtly shaded studies in color and dreamy landscapes.

Nowhere is the line between wearable art and fashion harder to draw than in France, which, as might be expected given the dominance of the fashion industry there, is not especially known for artwear. The artists and artisans who, in other circumstances, might be tempted to make wearable art are, in many cases, employed in supplying handmade textiles to the couture industry itself. There do exist small design houses on the edges of fashion, producing one-of-a-kind or limited-edition clothes from their own handmade textiles; the designer Sarah Aloïsi is a good example. Aloïsi, who studied and shows in France and in Japan, makes textiles, clothing, accessories, and objects using several techniques including felting, painting, and photo-transfer; she also makes clothes from paper. Like the New RenaisCAnce's work, Aloïsi's clothing, which is one-of-a-kind, is fashionable, concentrating as much on cut and line as on surface and showing a good deal of influence from Japanese designers like Miyake, but she shows it primarily in galleries. Given this blurring of the lines between artwear and fashion, it is surprising to discover that there is a wearable art competition in rural France that has little to do with fashion. The competition, called Atout Fil, is held annually in Vauvert, a small town in southeastern France located between Montpellier and Nîmes. Atout Fil, which also bills itself as *la folie du vêtement* (the madness of clothing), was founded in 1986

and is probably the oldest of the non-American wearable art competitions. Each year the show's organizers choose a theme to be reflected in the entries; past examples include "Party Clothes," "Space 3000," and "The Ten Commandments." The competition is open both to professionals and amateurs, and, though all entries are modeled, the organizers encourage entrants to concentrate on audacious, creative originality, not wearability. Staged as a single annual performance, Atout Fil gathers a substantial audience and modest corporate sponsorship; about six moderate cash prizes are awarded each year.[18]

Further examples at the flamboyant end of the European spectrum are works such as those spotlighted by Italian fashion designer Samuele Mazza for his single-garment series of books and accompanying exhibitions, which began with *Brahaus* (1992) and continued with *Cinderella's Revenge* (1993), *Spectacles* (1995), and *In the Bag* (1996). The books concentrate mainly on either conceptual art or current fashion; *Brahaus* comes the closest of the four to showcasing artwear. Mazza commissioned each bra, mainly from European artists and designers, and they are studies in a variety of surface design techniques —painting, appliqué, collage—and the use of unlikely materials. All two hundred of them— whether made from wrought iron, glass, bread, clocks, film, or cloth—are wearable (4.22). Also on the conceptual side, but maintaining a foot in wearability, is the work of artists like the Slovenian Anda Klancic, whose background in fashion design underpins her conceptual, yet technically wearable, embroidery-based pieces, such as *Recycled Shells* (1999) and *Embraced by Nature* (1999), a corsetlike garment whose lacy embroidery resembles the texture of a desiccated leaf.

Australia and New Zealand

Artwear in Australia and New Zealand became established in the late 1970s and 80s, respectively. Australia's small, primarily urban population was formed substantially by immigration, and influences from other countries and cultures have been crucial in the development of its crafts. Weaving in particular, which became very popular after World War II, was influenced by immigrants and visitors from the British Isles, Germany, and Scandinavia, while many native-born Australians, both then

4.18 opposite

WALTER BRIX German (b. 1965)
Hitoe Hosonaga (unlined kimono), 1998
Stiffened viscose, cotton, Chinese ink; calligraphy

Brix's work springs from his expertise in historic Japanese textiles and garments. Although his kimonos often incorporate new imagery and nontraditional materials such as synthetics, lacquer, and metal, they often radiate the elegant serenity of their antique Japanese counterparts.

4.19 – 4.20 previous page

ROLANDO RASMUSSEN working in Germany (b. Paraguay, 1942)
Triangelkleid, 1987
Painted silk

ELLEN EIS German (b. 1942)
Scarf, 1987
Painted silk

Both these pieces date from the period when silk painting was at the height of its popularity in Germany. Rasmussen's dress reflects the fashionable wedge silhouette of the period, while Eis's dramatic scarf can be worn however the wearer desires.

4.21 right

ROBIN GIDDINGS British
Jacket, 1984
Machine-embroidery on burnout fabric

This lacelike jacket was created by machine-embroidering on "Avalon," a fabric that disintegrates in water.

4.22 below

MONICA ZAULI Italian
Asburgico (Hapsburg), 1991
Wood and cloth

The Rococo-style gilt-frame cups of Zauli's wearable bra, featured in Samuele Mazza's book *Brahaus*, imply that their contents should be viewed as works of art.

and now, have studied abroad. This openness to outside influences has made Australian artists unusually active participants in the international textile and artwear community.

Wearable art was initiated in Australia in the 1970s by weavers and surface designers practicing techniques like tie-dye and batik. Batik was especially popular, perhaps because of the proximity of Indonesia, and it became not only a favorite surface design technique for white Australians but an important form both of self-expression and income for Aboriginal women. Beginning at least as early as 1973, when knitter Jenny Kee established her company Flamingo Park (4.23), a number of designers and craftspeople set up what were essentially small fashion houses making limited-edition, handmade, often ethnically flavored clothing and accessories—ponchos, scarves, coats, jackets, caftans—which tended to be categorized at the time as *art clothing* or simply as fashion. Grace Cochrane, in her history of Australian crafts, describes many as "small and often untrained producers" who were more interested in making the textile than designing the garment, and who

sold their wares through craft shops and galleries rather than boutiques or department stores.[19]

From these beginnings, an active and diverse group of artists emerged, practicing virtually every available textile technique. They created an impressive network of professional organizations, such as the Batik Association (later the Surface Design Association of Australia), the Fashion and Textile Designers Guild, and the South Australia Designers Collective, to help disseminate ideas and information and promote their work through conferences, workshops and classes, exhibitions, and performances. Museums also started to build up collections and set up exhibitions. One of the first shows was *Art Clothes*, mounted at the Art Gallery of New South Wales in 1980, and it was followed by many others, both domestic and traveling. *Australian Fashion: The Contemporary Art*, a 1989 show organized by The Powerhouse in Sydney (which toured to the Victoria & Albert Museum in London, and Japan and Korea in 1990 and 1991), typically focused on the *Australianness* of Australian artwear, which is characterized by a keen sense of

4.23 below left

JENNY KEE Australian (b. 1947)
Oz Outfit, 1986
Cotton, silk; hand-knitted, crocheted, printed

Kee, one of Australia's early artwear artists, has been hailed as a pioneer of a uniquely Australian style in textile design, based on its landscape, flora, fauna, and Aboriginal art.

4.24 below center

BARBARA ROGERS Australian (b. 1955)
African Notions, 1999
Silk georgette, kangaroo leather; shibori-dyed and discharged

Rogers is broadly influenced by the colors and patterns of African textiles, hence this piece's title. Her use of kangaroo leather for the sleeveless coat also links it to Australia.

4.25 below right

STEPHEN GALLOWAY Australian
Frill-necked Dress, 1989
Suede; machine-embroidered

Seventeenth-century Flemish embroidery inspired this chic dress, but the motifs are typically Australian—frill-necked lizards, beetles, snakes, and native flowers.

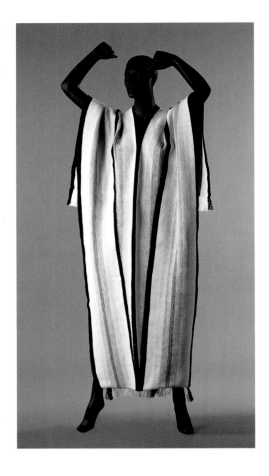

place (4.25). Many artists acknowledge that their work reflects either specific aspects of Australian culture or the light and colors, flora and fauna, of the landscape; and some, like the dyer Barbara Rogers, have worked with indigenous materials like kangaroo leather (4.24).

The idea of making art clothes, or handmade textiles, for production purposes seems to have been perfectly acceptable in Australia, and a number of highly respected makers—Jenny Kee, the weaver Liz Williamson, the screenprinter Linda Jackson, to name only three—engaged in it. Moreover, although many artists also make one-of-a-kind pieces, there seems to have been little interest, of the kind that exists in the United States, in making artwear that will hang on the wall as well as function on the body. Australian art clothing can be elegant, like Stephen Galloway's finely tailored, hand-embroidered dresses; vibrant, like Liz Williamson's cloth; or theatrical (4.28), like Patricia Black's freeform ensembles of yards of trailing, shibori-dyed silk, or Peter Tully's gray wool business suit covered with holograms—but there seems always to be the necessity of the body beneath and the consciousness and acceptance of the frame-work of fashion.

Artwear in New Zealand has a shorter history than it does in Australia, and for more than fifteen years it has been dominated by the Montana World of Wearable Art Awards (WOW®), which began in 1987 as the New Zealand Wearable Art Awards, and is held every September in Nelson. The first show was staged as a promotion for a local art gallery by sculptor Suzie Moncrieff, and it was successful enough to encourage her to repeat it the following year. WOW has grown into a large and sophisticated operation, with its own museum, which houses many of the competition's winning entries, and a plethora of corporate sponsors. It showcases and promotes artwear on an unparalleled scale and has become a major tourist attraction for Nelson, which is no mean achievement given how hard wearable art has struggled for recognition and reward elsewhere. Moncrieff's show is now a highly theatrical extravaganza in which up to several hundred fantastic garments are modeled with lights, music, and dance before audiences that number up to 2,500 per event.[20] Show entries, which come primarily from New Zealand but also from Asia, Britain, Europe,

Australia, and the United States, are juried by a panel of judges who accept between forty and sixty percent of the entries. In addition to the overall winner of the competition, cash prizes are also awarded in a number of subcategories such as Creative Excellence (open only to previous competition winners), Avant Garde, Illumination Illusion (garments that light up), and Bizarre Bra (4.27).[21] The website notes that a number of New Zealand artists and designers have launched their careers at WOW, and the competition offers participants plenty of publicity. Artists work within certain size restrictions (the 1999 entry form warned that garments could not exceed three meters in height and one-and-a-half meters in width lest they knock out the side lights on the catwalk) but otherwise may enter in any category and use virtually any material or technique. The garment must be wearable but need not be streetworthy since, as the category names would suggest, the WOW style of wearable art is exuberant, spectacular, and similar to performance art (though the artists do not model their own pieces) or theatrical costume. Its closest American counterpart is probably Friends of the Rag, discussed in Chapter 5, and there are parallels, too, with some of the promotional performances of the South Australian Designers Collective in the early 1980s and with Atout Fil. Artists are also free to submit quieter, more fashionlike entries, but they tend to be obscured by the more spectacular competition.

In WOW's wake, competitions have proliferated, in New Zealand and Australia in particular, providing additional opportunities both for theatrically minded artists who participate in WOW and for others whose work is more subdued. One directly WOW-inspired creation is the four-year-old Fashion Fantasia awards event in Hobart, Tasmania. Like WOW, it was created for promotional purposes by gallery owner Rossy Roberts-Thomson, who was inspired by Moncrieff's success. Its literature invites artists, craftspeople, and students to take fashion to its limits by regarding the body as a blank canvas on which to superimpose their ideas and aesthetic choices executed in any textile craft. Although the literature includes "saleable wearables" among the list of desired entries, the grand-prize winners to date have all leaned toward the more theatrical side of the genre.

4.26 opposite top

SHIN YOUNG-OK Korean (b. 1949)
One of Two, 1988
Cotton, silk; warp-face woven

Shin has been making artwear since 1980, though it is not now her primary artistic focus. This piece is based on a traditional ceremonial robe worn by Korean civil and military functionaries.

4.27 opposite bottom

DEBORAH QUAIFE New Zealand
Self Defence, 1988
Painted papier-mâché

This was the Supreme Award Winner (the grand prize) of the 1988 Montana World of Wearable Art Awards. It has several references to historic fashion—its silhouette is like a 1920s *robe de style*, and Yves Saint Laurent designed a dress with similar cone-shaped breasts for his 1967 African Collection.

4.28 right

PATRICIA BLACK Australian (b. 1956)
The Luminous Bardo, 1995
Silk; *itajime* shibori-dyed

This work, the 1995 Silk Section winner at the Montana World of Wearable Art Awards, is about transition and transformation, expressed through juxtaposed light, dark, and vibrant colors and the cocoonlike wrap of the silk around the body. The work's title is Tibetan Buddhist, and refers to the state of transition an individual experiences after death and before rebirth.

LEE, KI HYANG Korean
Nature, ca. 2000
Hand-painted fabric

This statuelike coat and headpiece represent Avalokitesvara Boddhisattva, or Kwan Yin, an enlightened Buddhist being closely associated with compassion and relief from suffering.

4.30 right

KIM, JUNG-HEE Korean
Beauty of Sack Dong, ca. 2000
Silk *nobang*; piecing

This piece appears based on the *chogori* and *ch'ima*, the short bodice and high-waisted pleated skirt of traditional Korean women's costume. *Saekdong* is a traditional combination of colors arranged in rainbow stripes according to ideas of yin, yang, and the five elements.

Korea and Japan

In *Fashion Asia*, Douglas Bullis explains that the idea of American-style artwear, in which elaborate, handcrafted garments are made to be hung on the wall, has never caught on in Asia because it runs counter to the tradition of packing one's finest garments away in chests to protect them from insects.[22] It is clear from the preceding survey of Australia and New Zealand that artwear need not, in fact, be intended for the wall. I would suggest instead that American-style artwear has not been correspondingly strong in Asia precisely because it so strongly reflects traditional Asian influences. During the period when wearable art was emerging in the West, the East was continuing to embrace and transform Western fashion; an anti-fashion movement energized by traditions that they had abandoned was unlikely to seem attractive. Since the 1980s, however, there has developed a small presence of what may legitimately be called artwear in Korea (4.26).

There are a number of artists working in studio fiber art in Korea and also in fashion design, and the idea of using their skills to make artwear seems to have been sparked by the exhibition *Art to Wear: New American Handmade Clothing*, which was organized by the American Craft Museum in 1984 and visited Korea in 1985. Chunghie Lee, who is unquestionably the most internationally known and successful Korean artist in this genre, was able to mount a solo exhibition of her crocheted wearable art in 1986, and in that same year the Korean National Museum of Contemporary Art put on the first of three exhibitions of garments made by Korean fiber artists and designers.

Wearable art remained quite active as an exhibition phenomenon through the 1990s.[23] The first Kwangju Biennale International Art to Wear Exhibition took place in 1995, accompanied by a handsome catalogue. Eighty-nine artists participated, sixty-four of them Korean, the balance invited from Europe, Japan, and North and South America. The Biennale has continued, and there is now a museum of wearable art in Kwangju filled with pieces that have been acquired from successive Biennales. There have also been touring exhibitions organized by the Korea Fashion and Culture Association (4.29), one in 1998 that went to Germany and *Air of the East: Fashion Art from Korea*, which traveled to three venues in the

United States in 2000–01 before going on to Nepal. In the exhibition catalogue introductions, the organizers of these exhibitions make it clear that their aims are promotional, either for the fashion industry, for the economy of the host city or institution, or for the influence and reputation of Korean art and fashion.[24] Artwear, however, has never moved beyond institutional exhibitions and universities into the wider culture. There are no galleries or boutiques in Korea that show or sell wearable art, and there is essentially no commercial market for it. Many practitioners teach in Korean universities and for them it seems to serve as a measurable achievement of their skill and creativity, almost in the same way that publications function for academics in the United States.[25]

Korean artwear appears as both traditional Korean garments (4.30) and Western fashionable forms (4.31), and uses as wide a variety of weaving and surface design techniques and materials as wearable art does anywhere else in the world. Some artists have also chosen to explore traditional Korean textile crafts, as Chunghie Lee has done with the piecing techniques known as *pojagi* (4.33).[26] Koreans receive rigorous training when they study textiles or fashion[27] and so their work is technically accomplished. But since there is no domestic commercial market for Korean

4.31 previous page

MYUNG HEE PARK Korean
Who Am I?, ca. 2000
Wool, polyester, sponge

Rather than East-West fusion, this jacket combines the tailoring of a man's coat with a woman's breasts.

4.32 right

JEUNG-HWA PARK working in U.S. (b. Korea)
Inspiration of Falling Woods, 2000; *Deep, Dark Leaves*, 1999
Merino wool, silk; knitted, felted, resist-dyed

Park seeks to embody in her firm yet soft textiles the principles of yin and yang, the merging of opposites. She transforms smooth, flat wool knit by shaping, stitching, dyeing, and felting into its opposite: a springy, textured, deeply three-dimensional object.

4.33 opposite

CHUNGHIE LEE Korean (b. 1945)
No-Name Woman, 2000
Silk *nobang*, pieced, *gekki* stitching

In the early 1990s Lee, formerly a crocheter, knitter, and felter, discovered *pojagi*, a traditional Korean patchwork wrapping cloth that is sewn with exquisite triple rows of stitches. Lee's fascination with *pojagi* transformed her artwear, and her use of it has led several non-Korean artists to begin to explore the technique as well.

wearable art, it need not actually be wearable. Some of it is, of course; but much, whether through the use of unusual materials or distorted forms, seems primarily conceptual, metaphoric, or sculptural in nature.

Japan is the source of many of the influences on artwear, but artwear has not gained much of a foothold in Japan. There are a number of likely reasons. Japan has a long history of fine textile craftsmanship, a strong contemporary fiber art movement, and an innovative textile industry that fuses traditional crafts techniques with twenty-first-century technology. Traditionally, Japan has recognized no divide between art and craft, and thus textile artists had no historical framework for trying to recontextualize clothing. The wave of feminism that swept much of the Western world in the 1960s and 70s and that underpinned the development of art to

wear did not then occur in Japan. The country's postwar embrace of Western fashion and the conformity of its culture may also have rendered it uninterested in an anti-fashion movement, and Japanese fashion designers' deft fusion of traditional Japanese and Western elements occupied the place that in the United States was occupied by artwear. Moreover, the 1980s—artwear's strongest decade—was the period when Issey Miyake and his Japanese cohorts held sway over high fashion, which may have further obviated the need for a countermovement. In fact, the most exciting textiles being made today in Japan are arguably those that the textile designers and companies Nuno, Junichi Arai, Jurgen Lehl, and Miyake Design Studio produce for the fashion industry. Both Lehl and Miyake make clothing from their textiles (Lehl also serves the furnishing industry), but Miyake,

while his artistry is unquestioned, is not the primary designer of the textiles he uses, although he works very closely with Makiko Minagawa, the textile designer for Miyake Design Studio.

There are Japanese fiber artists who have created an occasional kimono within a larger body of work in wall hangings and fiber sculpture, like Hiroyuki Shindo, Japan's renowned indigo dyer. There is also the prolific Itchiku Kubota, whose extensive series of kimono landscapes executed in stitch-resist (*tsujigahana*) and paste-resist (*yuzen*) techniques is legendary.[28] Kubota's focus was the re-creation of *tsujigahana*, a lost art that flourished in Japan during the fourteenth through the sixteenth centuries, and whose characteristic motifs and colors he adapted to contemporary taste. Kubota came from an older generation of Japanese

craftsmen who continued to work within the longstanding craft tradition and did not identify with artwear; his work, however, exhibits many of its hallmarks, particularly its concentration on technique. Kubota's kimonos are most often displayed on the wall, although in the catalogue of an exhibition mounted from his work in the mid-1980s, a number of his kimonos are shown in fashion-magazine-style photos being modeled by Caucasian women and men as if to link the kimonos explicitly with Western fashion.

There are also a handful of textile artists who sometimes explore the social and conceptual aspects of clothing using Western-style garments as part of a larger body of work that encompasses hangings and three-dimensional installation pieces. Their garments may or may not be wearable, according to the demands of each piece, and artists such as Suzumi Noda (4.35) may play with the contrast between wall-hung and worn pieces by showing pieces both on a wall and on a wearer within the same installation. Noda and her compatriots Noriko Narahira, who works with lacelike, open structures (4.36), Yoko Ishigaki, a dyer and embroiderer (4.34), and Michiko Kawarabayashi (1.6), who works with a variety of printing and fabric manipulation techniques, all exhibit their garments at a wide variety of Japanese venues such as Kyoto's Gallery Gallery, and exhibitions and competitions in Australia, Europe, and the United States.

The artist in Japan who seems to come to American-style artwear is Kyoto-based Jorie Johnson, a transplanted American who has been living in Kyoto since 1987. Johnson makes felt, which she discovered while studying in Finland in 1977, using an innovative layering technique allowing her to create representational motifs in the material, which she then uses for unusually shaped garments that are often conceptually keyed to the seasons (4.37). Perhaps the most unusual "wearable art" objects currently to be found in Japan are the embroideries created under the auspices of the Nui Project, a division of the textile workshop at Shobu Gakuen, a rehabilitation facility for the developmentally disabled in Kagoshima City. Fourteen Shobu Gakuen residents, under the supervision of two coordinators, embroider ready-made garments, primarily shirts, but also coats and dresses. The idea of using premade garments is to give some framework to the embroiderers' often wild creativity; the garments, thick with abstract stitches that have the obsessive quality that characterizes much outsider art, are both aesthetically compelling and wearable. The clothes, which are intended to be commercially saleable, have toured in a number of outsider art and design fairs around Japan, and have recently been shown for the first time in the United States.

4.34 opposite left

YOKO ISHIGAKI Japanese (b. 1978)
Hand Cover, 1999
Silk; wax-dyed, embroidered

Ishigaki aims to reconnect people with the primal senses and emotions that modern life blunts by superimposing on the surface of garments imagery that suggests the body's interior. These beautiful gloves, for instance, appear to be raw flesh.

4.35 opposite right

SUZUMI NODA Japanese (b. 1951)
Paper Soap Jacket, 1996
Paper soap, beads; pieced

Noda often uses commercial products or labels to pose questions about why we dress, and the relationships between our selves, our lives, and our clothes. This jacket is from her *Closed Clothes* series, which confronts issues of presence/absence, concealment and visibility, and memory.

4.36 opposite below

NORIKO NARAHIRA Japanese (b. 1948)
Lace Dress, ca. 2000
Silk; machine stitched

Narahira's wearable work generally utilizes Western garment forms. The whorls of machine stitching that constitute the lace of this figure-hugging dress appear simultaneously light and dense.

4.37 right

JORIE JOHNSON working in Japan
(b. U.S., 1954)
Catch a Falling Star from the *Aurora Borealis* series, 2002
Wool, holographic and polyester fibers, novelty yarn, metallic fabric; felted

Felt connotes comfort and protection, so Johnson's use of it for this spiky winter coat, hat, and spats seems particularly appropriate.

5

Stretching the Boundaries:Conceptual and Performance Pieces

5.1 below

ESTELLE AKAMINE American (b. 1954)
Red and Black Cocktail Dress, 1984
Screen, grommets, exterior enamel paint, rattan

Akamine spoofs fashion with costumes made from recycled and industrial materials. This dress appeared in *Akamine Bound*, a collaboration with the Footloose Dance Company.

5.2 opposite

KAISIK WONG American (1950–1990)
Blue and *Yellow/Green Rays*, from *The Seven Rays* series, 1974
Synthetic gauze, lamé, brocade; appliquéd

Created for performances at the Dalí Museum in Spain, these costumes incorporate references to Buddhist thought and the natural world that are difficult to decipher. The *Yellow/Green Ray*, however, clearly suggests an ear of corn.

Clothing-focused Performance Art

Artwear is intended mainly for formal or everyday wear, but a small group of artists who have made wearable art for these mainstream functions have also made it for use in performance art. Some, like Debra Rapoport, whose early series of wearable pieces called *Fibrous Raiment* (5.3) was used in performance, flirted only briefly with the genre, while others have concentrated on it. Artists have also occasionally designated for performance (by others) earlier works that were not made with that intent. For example, two kimonos made by Yoshiko Wada in the 1970s as explorations of ikat- and shibori-dyeing were subsequently lent to dancer Shizumi Manale to be used in dance performances. Artwear's near-universal theme of transformation and its inherent theatricality, seen in nonperformance works such as Joan Steiner's architectural garments or K. Lee Manuel's befeathered collars and capes, makes the genre a natural fit with performance (5.1). Although much of the performance art of the 1970s was conceptual, focused on ideas rather than costumes, performance-art chronicler RoseLee Goldberg has identified a performance subgenre that leans more towards entertainment and is wrapped up in contemporary culture[1]; and it is here that wearable art–based performance seems to fit most comfortably.

Kaisik Wong was involved in performance art early and, given the flamboyance of even his designs for street clothes, performance was a hospitable genre. Some of his first efforts were more traditionally theatrical, such as his work for the film *Messages Messages* (1968), made by the avant-garde filmmaker and photographer Steven Arnold, and the costumes for the stage show *Monkey and the White Bone Demoness* (1970), in which he also performed with the San Francisco drag troupe The Cockettes. Wong continued to perform, dramatizing his explorations of nature and his own ethnic heritage and search for enlightenment. His most ambitious undertaking was probably *The Seven Rays*, a series of grand ceremonial garments commissioned by Salvador Dalí (the two were introduced by a mutual friend in 1971) for the opening of the Dalí Museum in Figueras, Spain, in 1974, and which Wong and a company of his friends used in a series of street performances there (5.2). The series' enigmatic title refers to what Wong termed the seven rays of energy, and each piece functions at multiple symbolic levels. Each represents a color in the spectrum, which in turn relates to a vital center of the body. Wong also incorporated Buddhist thought, in which each color is ruled by an ascended master—an enlightened spiritual being who may act as a guide toward enlightenment to those still on earth—and each also has associations with ancient civilizations and aspects of the natural world, like corn, sun, and rain. Most often, though, Wong performed in the character of the Monkey King. Monkey is a powerful and unruly creature whose adventures during his search for enlightenment are told in a sixteenth-century Chinese allegorical folk tale. Wong performed as Monkey on many occasions—on stage, in parades, festivals, and fashion shows, and on the

5.3 right

DEBRA RAPOPORT American (b. 1945)
Rubber Labyrinth, 1970
Rubber; weft looping

Rubber Labyrinth is one of a series of
garments Rapoport called *Fibrous Raiments*,
which explore what happens when traditional
textile structures are combined with unlikely
materials.

5.4 opposite top

CORKY BROWN American (b. 1949)
The Coupon Coat, from *Alter Egos*, 1985
Mixed media

5.5 opposite center

DIANA AURIGEMMA American (b. 1946)
Portable Culture Coat and Carrying Case,
from *Traveling Modes and Devices*, 1978
Mixed media

5.6 opposite bottom

RUTH PELZ American (b. 1949)
Martian Fertility Goddess, from *Traveling
Modes and Devices*, 1978
Cotton, polyester, nylon, velvet

These three pieces by members of Seattle
performance troupe Friends of the Rag show
the group's range: a fashionlike *Coupon Coat*,
which recalls a nonwearable one made of
recycled product packaging by artist Mimi
Smith from the 1960s; a familiar wearable art
kimono-based coat, its long sleeves serving as
individual canvases for dyed and appliquéd
versions of famous paintings; and a fantasy,
many-breasted fertility goddess.

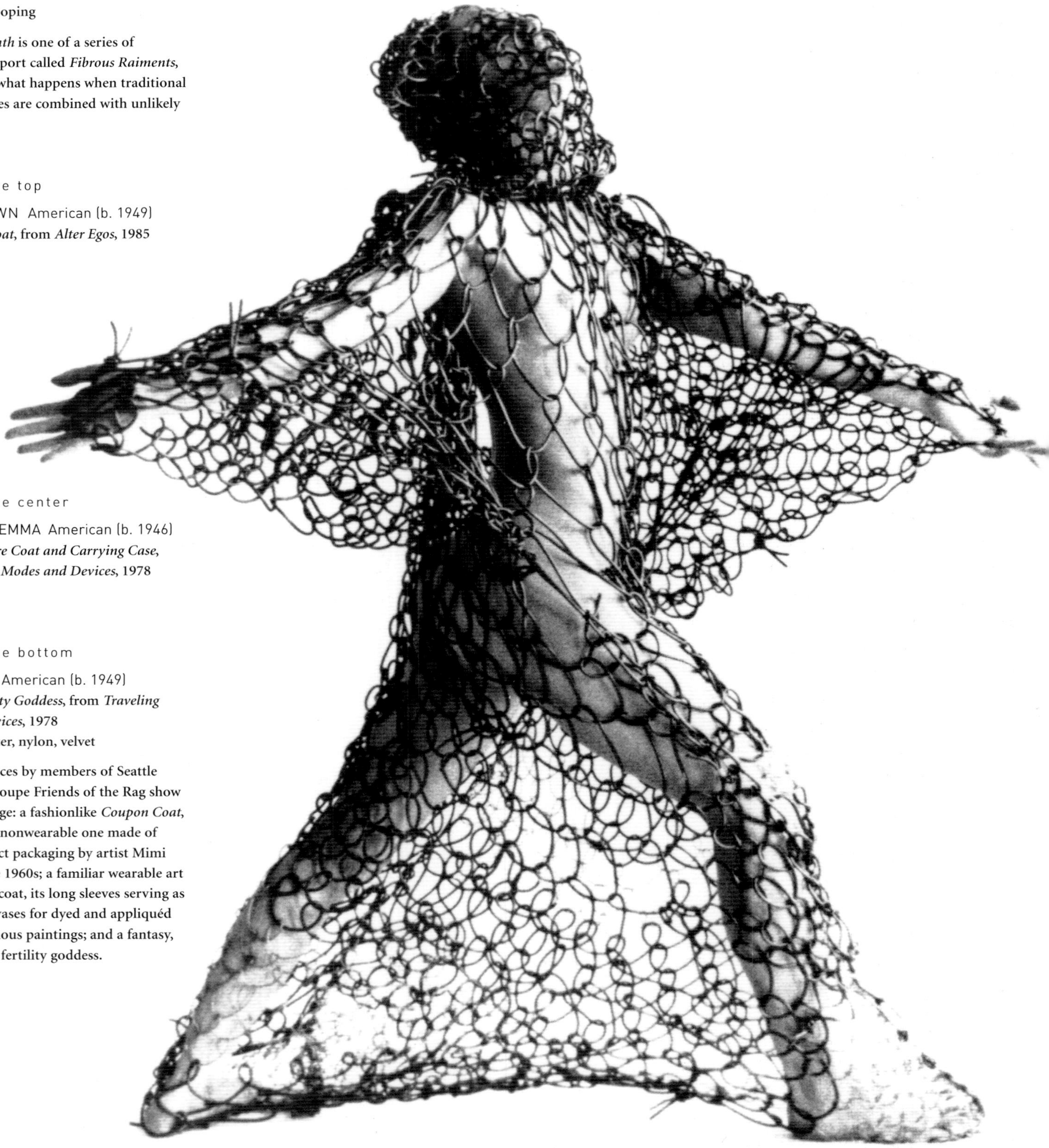

street. A gifted photographer who incorporated his pictures into the process of creation, Wong also photographed himself a number of times wearing different versions of the costume (5.7).

Among the few in performance who were formally aligned with artwear was Seattle's Friends of the Rag, a consortium of artists who performed in costume at bars, galleries, museums, festivals, and outdoors. Founded in 1972 by Mickey Gustin and Madeline Foster, they first performed at a fundraiser for presidential candidate George McGovern. The group quickly moved away from politics to focus instead on performance as a means of showing off the wearable art of each participating artist through short stage shows that were like dance concerts where each performer would move to music, and "platform" shows where the performers would circulate between a series of viewing platforms surrounded by their audience. Their performances were, in fact, akin to the nonrunway style of fashion show popular in both the United States and Europe prior to World War II,[2] although it is likely that none of the participants were aware of this. Friends of the Rag had a core membership of about fifteen artists who helped to plan each event; their numbers, however, could swell to as many as fifty, depending on the performance. Their early membership included a number of designers making fashionable clothes, accessories, and jewelry, but the group was best known for its more playfully outrageous costumes (5.6). Often their performances were commissioned by arts institutions for special events: they transformed themselves into musical instruments for the Seattle Symphony, Martians for the opening of the Seattle Art Museum's Andy Warhol exhibition, and living sculptures for the Henry Art Gallery. Their most ambitious undertaking was *Traveling Modes and Devices,* a small, juried touring exhibition mounted in 1978 by the Western Association of Museums that featured a dozen garments by nine artists. Friends of the Rag kicked off the tour with performances at the Smithsonian's Renwick Gallery and the White House in Washington, D.C., that included about half of the costumes in the exhibition augmented with additional pieces (5.5).

By 1979, Friends of the Rag had disbanded. They reassembled in 1984 with a substantially new group of artists, and with somewhat different goals and performance methods.

They remained artwear-driven and flamboyant, but whereas the earlier incarnation had usually welcomed anyone who wished to participate, with artists often performing their own work, the later Friends of the Rag vetted all pieces submitted for performances, which were collaborations between the artists and professional choreographers and dancers who were hired to stage and realize the events. Like the first group, the second Friends of the Rag lasted about seven years and reassembled occasionally thereafter; their last performance was in 1994 (5.4).

An artist currently active in performance is Nick Cave. In some ways, Cave's career parallels Kaisik Wong's: he created a very successful line of men's and women's one-of-a-kind and limited-edition wear, which he and his partner Jeffrey Roberts sold at their own store, Robave, in Chicago (now closed) (5.9). This aspect of his work, which is based on his beautiful hand-dyed and printed textiles, is very much in the artwear mainstream, and Cave continues to make it. But Cave is equally well known for his performance work, especially the *Sound Suit* series, which has been ongoing since the late 1980s and now numbers well over a hundred pieces. Cave's performance work is fueled by his experience as an African American man in the United States. Made from found, humble, and recycled materials like twigs, plastic tags, and bottle caps, the enveloping costumes he creates simultaneously and paradoxically suggest his African heritage and American stereotypes of blacks, while allowing him to completely conceal or change his identity. Cave performs both alone and with others, sometimes with scripted content and sometimes improvising; the content and focus of the performance will vary depending on who is on stage. Cave chooses his materials for a *Sound Suit* as much for their aural properties as their visual and metaphoric ones, so that as the costume moves in performance it will add its own sound to the accompanying music, song, and speech (5.10).[3]

There are also a few performance artists who do not make artwear as street or special occasion wear or for display, but who have produced a body of performance work that is so reliant on the garment and its materials that it merits inclusion here. Among them are Robert Kushner and Pat Oleszko, both of whom came to prominence in the 1970s.

5.7 above

KAISIK WONG American (1950–1990)
Self-Portrait as Monkey King, 1980s
Gelatin silver print

One of the many versions of Kaisik Wong dressed as the character of the Monkey King.

5.8 right

ROBERT KUSHNER American (b. 1949)
Pineapple Falsies, from *Robert Kushner and Friends Eat Their Clothes*, 1972
Pineapples, lady apples, chestnuts, cranberries, grapefruit

Kushner's spoof of Carmen Miranda's outrageous movie headgear is one of sixteen costumes created for his second edible-clothing performance. The showgirllike outfit is both titillating and discreet.

Kushner is best known today as a painter, one of the leaders of the Pattern and Decoration movement, but performance was his primary endeavor through much of the 1970s and costume was its focus. Like many of the artists who gravitated to artwear, Kushner grew up in an environment that was appreciative of textiles and clothing, and the materials that enlivened his childhood formed the basis for his costumes.[4] His performance work explores a whole range of cultural ideas about ritual, gender, beauty, fashion, sexuality, art, and the impact of both the clothed and nude body, and, in common with the broad thrust of wearable art, was shaped by his interest in the dress of both Western and non-Western cultures. It has also been noted that his costumes sprang from his struggle to reconcile the conflicting demands of the conceptual art movement in which he was trained and his desire as an artist to create beautiful objects.[5]

Kushner's performances were essentially fashion shows staged in galleries. The artist often played the role of emcee-cum-model, providing a mock-fashion-show commentary on the humorously titled and outrageously revealing or otherwise over-the-top clothes parading down the "runway" on models—often the artist's friends—who were obviously naked beneath their costumes. An excellent example of his style is *Robert Kushner and Friends Eat Their Clothes* (1972), one of several pieces that incorporated food (5.8).[6] Kushner, assisted by his models, made triballike garments from supermarket snacks, meats, and other produce, carefully choosing items—artichokes, celery, bread, hot dogs, fruit leather, and pretzels—that would make the clothes "attractive, appealing, appetizing, provocative, and piquant"[7]; they had to be all this as well as sturdy enough to wear. At the gallery the costumes were hung, like paintings, on the wall and then donned by the naked artist and his friends and modeled. At the end of the show, the models and the audience were, in conceptual art parlance, directed to "de-materialize" the art by eating the clothes directly off themselves and each other.

Kushner's later costumes embodied the same blend of beauty, humor, fashion, and cultural anthropology, but used more durable and often more traditional materials. Most were centered around the concept of a "line"—as in a designer's line of clothing—such as *The*

Winter and Spring Line (1973), *The New York Hat Line* (1975), and *The Persian Line* (1975–76) (5.11). The latter featured fifty-five flowing costumes inspired by the Iranian chador, for which Kushner painted the fabric. The piece reflected Kushner's desire to "seduce and transport the audience with fabric,"[8] which shows him in tune philosophically with mainstream wearable art. It also, perhaps more than any of his earlier works, underscores the tension between modesty and titillation and the role that clothing plays in each. Kushner did a few scattered performances following *The Persian Line* and he subsequently created clothing with both the Fabric Workshop and Crown Point Press, but by 1980 he was working primarily as a painter.

It is hard to categorize Pat Oleszko's work, which is a bawdy and satiric amalgam of sculpture, theater, dance, language, and popular culture expressed through both her costumed and naked body. The artist herself has characterized her role as "play[ing] the fool —in the sense of one who traverses cultures and interprets them for others."[9] When she began, in the late 1960s, Oleszko was attempting to make large-scale sculpture that explored the relation between people's lives and ideas and their bodies, using her own body as an armature. Like Kushner, Oleszko's work was not necessarily in tune with the period's prevailing conceptual art ethos but it attracted the attention of the crafts world, and she credits Paul Smith of the American Craft Museum with giving her career a boost when, in 1972, the museum hosted an early piece about female stereotypes, *New Yuck Woman*.[10] In piece after piece, Oleszko has used her circuslike costumes to transform herself into a staggering array of objects and characters (she has subdivided herself into as many as six at once), ranging from the roaming Statue of Liberty (*Liberty's A-Broad*) to a New York taxi (*Taxidermiss*), to a Picasso still-life (*Pat's Picasso*), to a plump trio of primary-colored Motown singers (*The Padettes of P.O. Town*) (5.12). Oleszko has also moved beyond solo live performance to outdoor installations— happenings that involve her audience, film, and video.

Oleszko's work is not akin to artwear in her use of materials, which are neither handcrafted nor precious. Her costumes were made of stretch fabrics over a cane structure and were built to

5.9 previous page top

NICK CAVE American (b. 1959)
Suit, 2002–03
Human hair, cotton, ball chain, leather

5.10 previous page bottom

NICK CAVE American (b. 1959)
Sound Suits, 2004
Found beaded and sequined garments;
de- and reconstructed

Cave, one of the few working in this genre to
create clothes for men, is also one of the few
making artwear both for the street, such as the
suit (top) that he wears on special occasions,
and for performance (bottom).

5.11 above

ROBERT KUSHNER American (b. 1949)
Purple, from *The Persian Line I*, 1974
Acrylic on taffeta, printed cotton, tassels

Kushner models a lavishly painted costume
based on the Iranian chador, an enveloping
garment worn by women. Particularly in the
context of male dress, it reveals what, in
Western fashion, is often hidden and conceals
what is normally visible.

5.12 opposite

PAT OLESZKO American (b. 1947)
The Padettes of P.O. Town, 1976
Mixed media

Fractured language and wordplay characterize
Oleszko's edgy, satiric work, and she often
plays multiple characters simultaneously. With
the Padettes, the Detroit-born Olesko turns
herself into a primary colored mixed-race trio
"danc[ing] to Motown hits in perfect sync,
without rehearsal." Oleszko is "the dummy in
the middle."

5.13 above

PAT OLESZKO American (b. 1947)
Coat of Arms and *The Handmaiden (Japan)*, 1975
Mixed media

Coat of Arms (left) is Oleszko's signature piece.
Its companion, *The Handmaiden*, was created
for a striptease performance in which Oleszko
removed one arm at a time while "recit[ing]
every conceivable pun on arms and armor."
Here, they are in tableau with the "cast-off sows
and together forever in true arm-mour."

stand up to repeated use and a lot of travel. More recently, she has been making inflatables, which allow her to make lightweight costumes and set pieces that are truly enormous. The link with artwear comes through the intersection of ideas and language. Oleszko looks upon words as objects, symbolic of ideas[11]; virtually all her work incorporates fractured language and puns that are at once funny and thought-provoking. That same playful literalness can also be found in artwear. Oleszko's style of humor, shown in pieces such as her signature *Coat of Arms* (5.13), a black jacket sprouting multiple arms pointing wildly in all directions, is echoed in many wearable artworks, among which are Teresa Nomura's *Keep Your Sunny Side Up* (1983) (5.14), a strapless cocktail dress fashioned as a table that sports a sunny-side-up egg plastered over each breast; Norma Minkowitz's *Sit on It* (1980), a crocheted hat in the form of a nesting bird; and Jody Pinto's *Hair Shirt* (1978) (5.15), a pigskin tunic silkscreened with luxuriant chest and underarm hair.

Garment as Metaphor

Unwearable wearable art sounds like an oxymoron, and to a degree it is. Because dress is full of sly, subjective meaning that we decode, often unconsciously, as it is worn, the removal of its functionality can allow us to view and analyze it objectively. Certainly, ever since Joseph Beuys hung his first *Felt Suit* (1970)

on the wall, unwearable dress has been an increasingly popular component of contemporary art. At the same time, fashion itself has become a subject for serious study and theorizing. Unwearable art usually focuses on the symbolic nature of dress, and, as Anne Hollander has noted, when dress is taken seriously it is usually because it is being treated as a metaphor or illustration, so one can comfortably focus on what clothes mean about something else instead of grappling with the messy subject of fashion itself.[12] So unwearable art, which frequently addresses issues of identity, loss, and gender or sexuality, may be regarded as a way of acknowledging the importance of dress and exploiting certain of its aspects—its intimacy, accessibility, familiarity, and wealth of symbolic meanings—while, like wearable art, avoiding fashion.

Although the majority of the artists who use symbolic, three-dimensional dress in their work do not also make artwear and most artists who make wearables make only the occasional unwearable piece if any at all, wearables and unwearables, in my opinion, are related in that both may use the garment as metaphor. Any artist who has made a piece that he or she envisioned both worn on the body and displayed hanging on the wall or freestanding like sculpture has considered a functionless role for the work; in that sense, wearable art has long flirted with the objectification of the garment. Balancing the many artists who feel their work is

5.14 above

TERESA NOMURA American (b. 1951)
Keep Your Sunny Side Up, 1983
Appliquéd cotton chintz, bead embroidery

This cocktail dress in the form of a cozy breakfast table uses eggs and bacon as coy reminders of the body it is concealing.

5.15 left

JODY PINTO American (b. 1942)
Created in collaboration with the Fabric Workshop and Museum
Hair Shirt, 1978
Pigment on pigskin

Pinto's pun recasts the hair shirt from a form of self-punishment to a supple leather tunic sprouting luxuriant underarm and chest hair. When worn by the (female) artist, it also suggests the discomforting mixing of gender roles and signals.

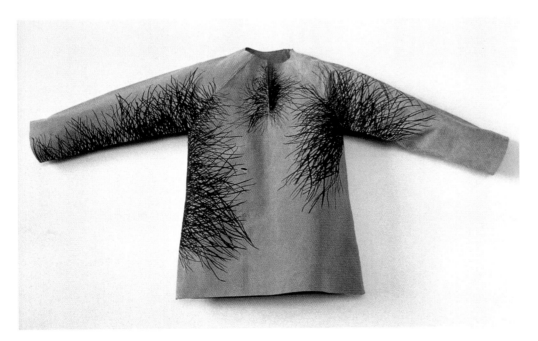

complete only when it is worn are those who are not particularly interested in making their art wearable. Nicki Hitz Edson likely spoke for many others when she said, "My main interest is not in whether [my kimonos] are wearable, but in the surface and the techniques of the work itself."[13] The idea of the body plainly remains important (else why make a garment?) but the active participation of a wearer is not always required.

Unwearable pieces by wearable artists are usually made so that technically they could be donned although in reality they cannot. Sometimes it is a matter of scale; Tim Harding (5.18), Yvonne Porcella (5.17), and Judith Content are among those who have made oversized pieces, especially kimonos, that are either slightly or obviously too large to be worn comfortably. This lends them a certain monumentality—Porcella's larger-than-life patchwork and appliqué kimonos were inspired by the oversize, kimono-shaped, and padded bedcovers called *yogi,* so that they also bear the same connotations of warmth and comfort as a traditional patchwork quilt.[14] Artists working only in metaphoric garments, not wearables, also use very large or small scale in works whose expression relies on either the absence of the body or connotations related to size, as is the case with Beverly Semmes's enormous, sensual, gallery-filling dresses and Charles Le Dray's smaller-than-normal men's suits, both exploring issues of gender and power. In other cases, un-wearability is mandated by the materials (5.31).

5.16 above

GLEN KAUFMAN American (b. 1932)
If The Glove Fits, Wear It, Baby, 1984
Mixed media

Kaufman's glove series of the mid-1980s ranged from quiet to glamorous and explored a wide variety of surface design techniques and visual puns.

5.17 right

YVONNE PORCELLA American (b. 1936)
Diamonds on Ice, 1984
Silk; painted, airbrushed, appliquéd, quilted

Porcella, known for her intense color combinations, chose an unusually subdued palette for this oversized kimono.

5.18 opposite

TIM HARDING American, (b. 1950)
Shroud #5, 1992
Cotton; collage-layered, quilted, slashed, frayed

Harding is alive both to textiles' relative fragility and what he calls their "culturally ingrained preciousness," which forbids us from damaging our "good" clothes. His work regularly violates this prohibition. Harding's slashed shroud, with its coffinlike central image is slightly oversized, which would make it challenging to wear.

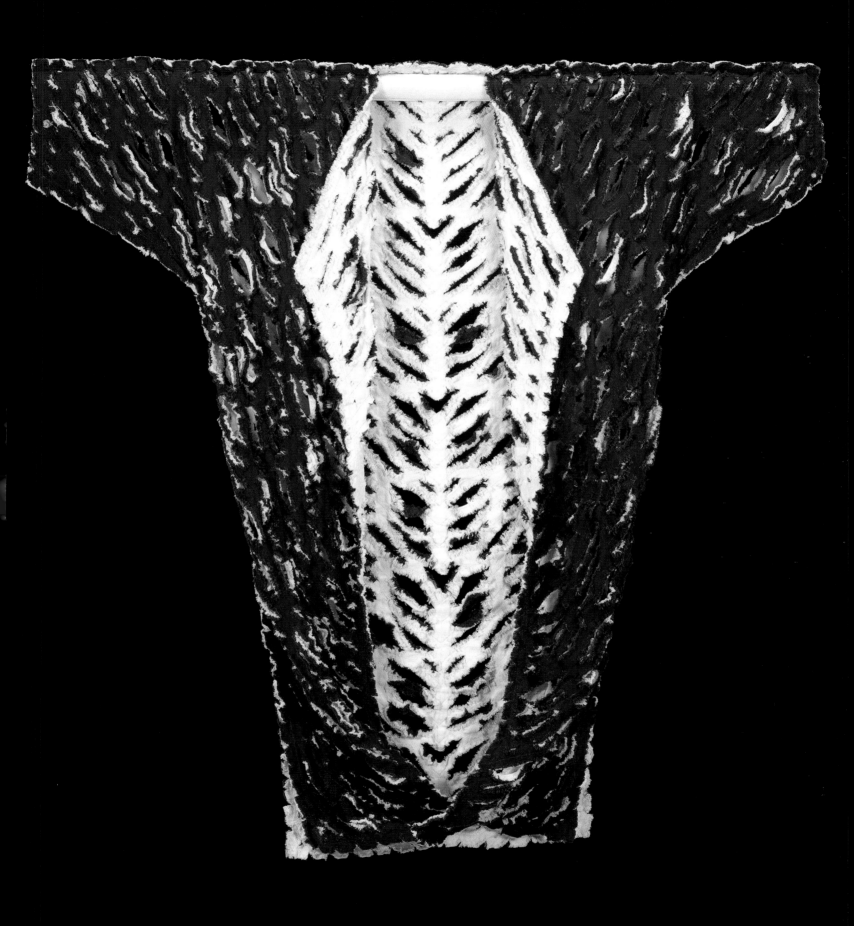

5.19 below

MARIAN SCHOETTLE American
(b. 1954)
When Push Comes to Shove, from the
Nightwalk series, 1996
Cotton; embroidered

The seven *Nightwalk* series dresses are about
evoking and confronting the fears of walking
alone at night. The route that wanders over
the dress was taken from an aerial photograph
of New York's Central Park.

5.20 right

RISË NAGIN American (b. 1950)
In Remembrance, 1983
Wool and silk appliqué

Nagin made this powerful mourning dress
as a gift for gallery owner and patron
Helen Drutt to commemorate the death
of her husband.

5.21 – 5.22 opposite

GAZA BOWEN American (1944–2005)
The Little Woman's Night Out, 1987 (above),
and *The American Dream*, 1990 (below), from
the *Shoes for the Little Woman* series
Mixed media

The common household cleaning
commodities and kitchen tools from which
Bowen made her breakthrough series of
shoes examining women's lives and roles in
American culture render all but *The American
Dream* impossible to wear. Instead, Bowen
rendered those shoes undesirable by choosing
an outmoded style.

In the late 1980s, Gaza Bowen chose to divorce
her work from wearability because the materials
that would imbue pieces with the desired
content were too fragile to be worn. Her *Shoes
for the Little Woman* series (5.21, 5.22), for
instance, could never be walked in, yet she made
the shoes just as she would any functioning pair
of shoes, often on a last that fitted her foot. Lack
of wearability may also be mandated by content
—certain meanings that an artist may be unable
or unwilling to convey in a work that either they
or someone else will wear, or that potential
wearers would be unwilling or unlikely to don.
Works about anger or grief created in reaction
to a direct experience can often—though not
always—fall into this category as too weighty,
too painful, or too personal for someone else's
self to be wrapped in (5.20).

A substantial number of artists outside the
United States also work with unwearable art.
One of the best known is the British artist
Caroline Broadhead, whose work evolved from
a basis in jewelry in the 1970s to address
ideas about clothes and the body, first through
disembodied garment parts stripped of
ornamentation—cuffs, sleeves, veillike collars—
and then via out-of-proportion garments like
Twin Shirts, two long, opposed T-shirts invisibly
conjoined at what would have been their hems;
and *Wraparound Shirt*, a straitjacketlike garment
with seven sleeves, which could physically be
worn but which defied conventional notions
of putting on and wearing (5.23). Gradually,
Broadhead, who was concentrating on exploring
ideas of presence and absence, freed herself from
the body, beginning with a series of sketchy,
wall-hung "garments" made only of their
connected seams. She subsequently produced
a series of ghostly, freestanding or suspended
dresses that cast their own substantial shadows
and appear paradoxically filled with absent,
slightly distorted bodies (5.24).[15] Broadhead's
plain white textiles are carefully chosen but are
rarely embellished with anything other than
seams. In its focus on form over surface, her
work is more reminiscent of some aspects of
avant-garde fashion—particularly the work of
Issey Miyake and Isabel and Ruben Toledo—
than it is of conventional artwear. American
artist Marian Schoettle was an associate of
Broadhead's in London in the 1980s; her
conceptual work from that time explores
similar themes, also through sheer, plain white
garments, as in her *Clothing Enigma* series,
that may be donned but appear impossible
to wear (5.25). Schoettle is one of the few
conceptual artists who also makes artwear,[16]
which she manages to infuse with some of
the conceptual rigor of her display pieces
(5.19); London-based Susie Freeman, whose
Pharmacopoeia project is discussed in Chapter
4, is another.

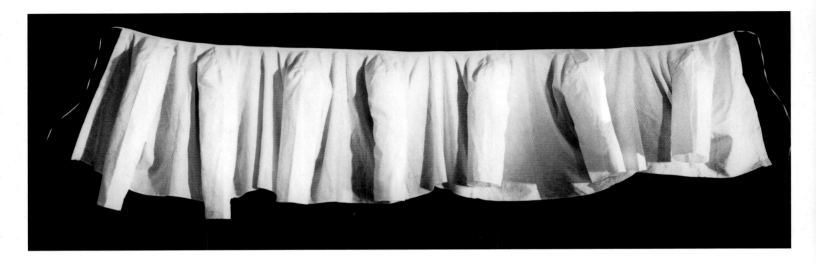

5.23 above

CAROLINE BROADHEAD British (b. 1950)
Wraparound Shirt, 1983
Cotton

Broadhead's unnerving but wearable shirt
suggests the warmth and security of swaddling,
as well as the straitjacketlike discomforts of the
restraint it imposes.

5.24 right

CAROLINE BROADHEAD British (b. 1950)
Wobbly Dress, 1992

Broadhead's series of ghostly, slightly distorted,
freestanding garments appear paradoxically
filled with invisible bodies. They are a small
part of a substantial series of works in which
Broadhead explores ideas of presence and
absence.

5.25 opposite

MARIAN SCHOETTLE American (b. 1954)
Double Shirt, from the series *Clothing Enigmas*,
1985
Silk mousseline

Schoettle's conceptual garments for installation
and performance promoted new ways of
thinking about clothes and their relationship
to the body. Like Caroline Broadhead's
Wraparound Shirt (above), Schoettle's double
shirt skewers conventional notions about how
garments should be put on and worn and the
power clothes exert over the body.

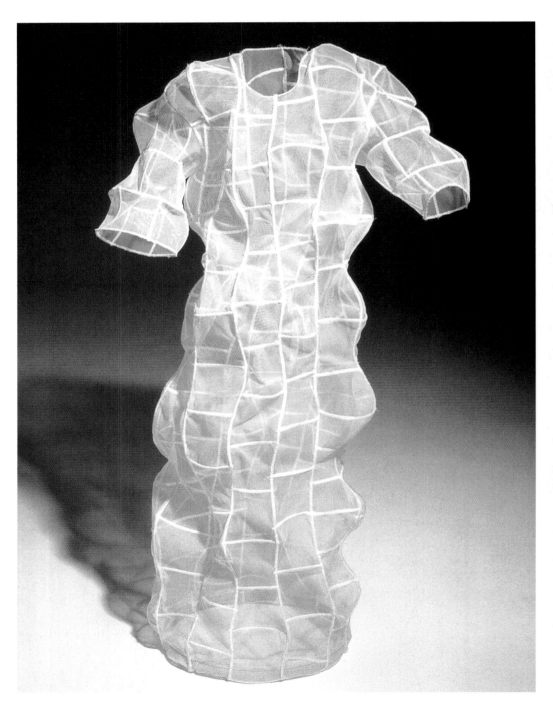

Irrelevant

5.26 above

Judith Shea at the Fabric Workshop in 1977. On the wall behind Shea are her *Semaphore Shirts* (top), paper jacket, and pants for *Four Continents*. The patternlike geometric cut, particularly of the shirts, suggests the influence of sources like Burnham's *Cut My Cote* and Tilke's *Costume Patterns and Designs*.

5.27 below right

DIANE JACOBS American (b. 1966)
Untitled (Red Hat), 1998
Letterpress on paper

The association of scarlet with sin is reinforced by the words—most euphemisms for sex or prostitute—printed on the thin strips of paper from which this floppy hat is woven. The hat is not intended to be worn, but its form implies wearing, and perhaps identifying oneself with or by these words.

5.28 opposite

JON ERIC RIIS American (b. 1945)
Heart of Gold Female #2, 2002
Tapestry-woven silk and metallic thread

Riis's T-shaped jacket symbolizes the body and the contradictory nature of clothing that simultaneously conceals and reveals it. The jacket's surface represents both skin and a covering garment cut away to show it, and it opens to reveal a woven image of the body's vital organs surrounded by blood-red tissue.

Artists usually use the "empty dress" as a conceptual trope (5.28), displaying it on the wall hanging from a hanger or hook, on an invisible mount, or, less frequently, on a headless mannequin or dress form. The anonymous mounting style leaves the identity of the theoretical wearer of the garment as an open question, one which seems especially attractive for art that aims to explore questions of identity, often from a feminist or minority perspective (5.27). Clothing is a natural fit with this perspective, since dress has historically been one of the few ways open to women and minorities to express themselves artistically or culturally. The feminist aspect of this kind of art as it developed in the 1970s shared both impulses and conventions with artwear, including the desire of women to challenge the male art establishment by making art in forms and from materials like textiles that spoke to female concerns and history, and the use of a nonfashion approach. Both this kind of feminist art and wearable art have been identified as reactions against the strict purity demanded by Minimalism.[17]

The painter Miriam Schapiro, a founder of the Pattern and Decoration movement, is probably the artist aligned most closely with artwear. Related to her feminist agenda was Schapiro's wish, like so many others, to dissolve the barriers between art and craft since women's work had traditionally been relegated to craft status.

Her large-scale celebratory kimono and fan *Femmages*[18] of the 1970s and early 80s, which were made of collaged and painted textiles glued to a canvas (5.29), were riotously colored and patterned, and borrowed imagery and technique from traditional women's textiles like quilting and crochet. Judith Shea, whose early training was in fashion design, also based her early, Minimalism-inspired work around non-fashion clothing. Her 1970s series of *Clothing Constructions* were simple, prefashion Western garments, like the *Semaphore Shirts* she made at the Fabric Workshop in 1977 that look like patterns right out of Dorothy Burnham's *Cut My Cote* (5.26). Also in common with much artwear was the *Clothing Constructions*' display method, which was to be hung on the wall from dowels.[19] Mimi Smith, whose empty clothing customarily dangles from hangers, dared to use fashionable forms coupled, like Bowen's shoes, with startling materials, such as the steel wool that trims both a nylon and lace peignoir (1966) (5.32) and the elegant pinstriped woman's suit in *Slave Ready* (1991), and the convex viewing window salvaged from an old washing machine inserted in the tummy of *Maternity Dress* (1966).

Adrian Bannon's *Thistledown Coat* (1998), which closely resembles a modified artwear kimono, is among the relatively few unwearable works that use the kimono form. Unwearables do often employ nonfashion garments as a sign

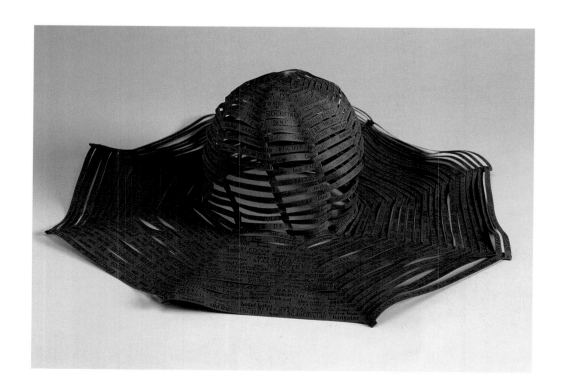

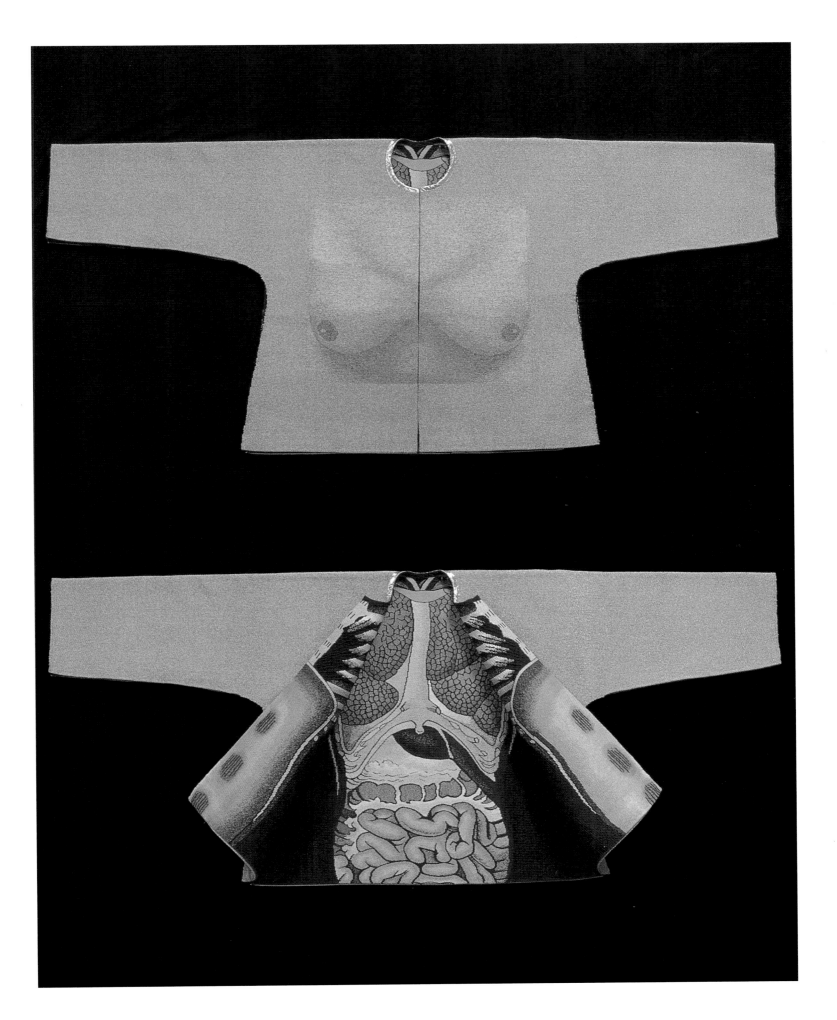

5.29 above

MIRIAM SCHAPIRO American (b. 1923)
Kimono, 1976
Fabric collage and oil on canvas

A characteristic Schapiro *Femmage*, with collaged textiles and paint forming the image of a kimono.

5.30 right

MARIAN SCHOETTLE American (b. 1954)
Contour Couture from the *Navigation* series, 1999–2004
Rayon; embroidered

Schoettle's artwear is both extremely wearable and strongly conceptual. *Contour Couture*, one of an edition of fifty, is a map dress, its topography charted by the line of white thread spiraling continuously around the dress from hemline to neckline.

5.31 opposite

CAROL LEE SHANKS American (b. 1957)
Ritual Tunic with Spine, 1997
Linen, banana fiber, plant pods, twigs; assembled

Shanks mainly makes wearables, but occasionally creates a piece intended only for the wall.

of seriousness, but since function has been removed from the equation, the concept of nonfashion can extend to fashionable forms that are simplified or no longer in use but still recognizable to the viewer. Several of Christine LoFaso's garments, especially her corsets and 1950s maternity skirts made of tea-dyed paper printed with text, fall into this category (5.33). So do Beverly Semmes's huge dresses, which conform to Empire style, first fashionable at the turn of the nineteenth century and revived periodically in the twentieth. Ironically, given their size, the proportions of her dresses, with their relatively short bodices and much longer skirts, are also commonly found in little girls' dresses. Jana Sterbak has also used simplified and out-of-fashion garments, including the crinoline (a mid-nineteenth-century hooped petticoat used to give skirts a characteristic bell shape) and the straight, sleeveless shift often worn as casual dress in the 1960s, which appears in her most famous piece, *Vanitas: Flesh Dress for an Albino Anorexic* (1987). Unwearable art also differs from wearable art in its customary focus on symbol over beauty in its artist-made materials, and sometimes the textiles are ready-made. Yinka Shonibare, a British-born, Nigerian-

raised Londoner, creates set pieces of ethnic-seeming textiles styled like eighteenth- and nineteenth-century Western fashions to explore issues of colonialism, race, and cultural identity. Shonibare's work turns on the scrambled history and associations of so-called Dutch Wax cloth, colorful resist-dyed textiles inspired by Indonesian batik that are actually mass-produced in Europe and marketed to and popular among resident, expatriate, and foreign-born Africans as a symbol of African identity and pride.[20] Almost alone among this group of artists, Shonibare makes neither the cloth nor the costume himself; he buys the cloth at markets in Britain and has the costumes made by a theatrical costumer. Sterbak's *Vanitas* is not beautiful but the (communal) process of making it is integral to the work: the shift is made of sixty pounds of salted, pounded flank steak and the owner or borrower is responsible for re-creating it according to the artist's instructions every time the piece is shown.

Shifting Boundaries

Wearable and unwearable art have a lot in common, and the line between them plainly

is porous. Moreover, as the boundaries between artwear, fashion, and art have shifted over the past generation, the issue of wearability versus concept has provided a continuing source of creative tension and challenge for designer, artist, and prospective wearer. Fashion has moved in a more conceptual direction in the hands of Japanese and European designers such as Miyake, Kawakubo, Hussein Chalayan, and Martin Margiela, who experiment with both cut and materials. And at present, a number of artists are engaging with the ambiguity between wearable and unwearable in much the same way, through more fashionable shapes and materials like

candy wrappers, can labels, recycled underwear, straight pins, and shredded currency, and through imagery that is often self-reflective. Their work may be edgier, but the desire to create for the body appears to be the same as that felt by wearable art's first generation. Unlike Schapiro and Shea, who carefully avoided any possibility of wearability so that their work might be taken seriously as art, this new artwear takes on the risk of function, although willing wearers other than the artists may be hard to find. Fortunately, as Miyake himself said in 1982, "The issue is not whether these clothes are worn or not. What counts is communication."[21]

5.32 following spread, left
MIMI SMITH, American (b. 1942)
Steel Wool Peignoir, 1966
Steel wool, nylon, lace
Smith incorporates household cleaning materials into garments to comment on women's lives and roles in contemporary American culture.

5.33 following spread, right
CHRISTINE LOFASO, American (b. 1950)
Redress: Gestation Corset, 1992
Paper, mink fur, metal, catnip-stained lacing, text from "Dora/A Case Study of Hysteria" by Sigmund Freud
Gestation Corset (non-wearable) is based on a nineteenth-century maternity corset.

Notes

Chapter 1

1 Nancy A. Corwin, "The Kimono Mind: Japonisme in American Culture," in Stevens and Wada, eds., *The Kimono Inspiration*, 30. Corwin notes the irony of the Western conviction that Japanese crafts embodied the preindustrial golden age for which the West was nostalgic, when in fact Japan was abandoning handcrafts in favor of industrialization.

2 Parry, ed., *William Morris*, 224.

3 Cunningham, *Reforming Fashion*, 12.

4 Quoted in Schweiger, *Wiener Werkstätte*, 209.

5 Cunningham, *Reforming Women's Fashion*, 187–188.

6 Fortuny's company, which established branches in Paris and New York during his heyday in the 1920s, continued to make Delphoses until 1952, three years after his death, under the management of his American distributor, Elsie Lee Gozzi. The Paris branch closed during World War II but the New York branch has become the company's main office, selling furnishing fabric made by the Fortuny factory in Venice.

7 De Osma, *Fortuny*, 94.

8 Morano, *Sonia Delaunay*, 21.

9 For an extensive discussion of the textile department at the Bauhaus, see Weltge, *Women's Work*.

10 Ibid., 42.

11 Corwin, in *The Kimono Inspiration*, 68, 73. Uehara advertised regularly in craft magazines like *Fiberarts* and *American Craft* and gathered a clientele from all over the United States, Canada, Britain, Germany, and Iran. Uehara continued to operate the Orizaba Company from Honolulu until 1988; in 1991 she moved to Los Angeles and reopened her business as the Texuba Co.

12 Ibid., 64–65.

13 Hollander, *Sex and Suits*, 17–18.

14 For an excellent discussion of the history of kimono in Western fashion, see Stevens and Wada, eds., *The Kimono Inspiration*.

15 "Body art" is now more commonly a reference to tattoo.

16 Conversation with Julie Schafler Dale, 13 January 1999.

17 Conversation with Jean Williams Cacicedo, 6 January 1999.

Chapter 2

1 Milinaire and Troy, *Cheap Chic Update*, 9.

2 Conversation with Candace Kling, 6 January 1999.

3 Conversation with Janet Lipkin, 22 August 1999.

4 Ibid.

5 Conversation with Janet Lipkin, 6 January 1999.

6 Conversation with Jo Ann Stabb, 9 August 1999.

7 See Wada, Rice, and Barton, eds., *Shibori*, 7.

8 Wada returned to Japan in the late 1970s for eighteen months in order to study shibori; she is now unquestionably one of the world's experts.

9 The Shibori Society, which in 1992 was absorbed into The World Shibori Network. See Wada, *Memory on Cloth*, 92.

10 Smith et al, *Body Covering*, 3.

11 Conversation with Julie Schafler Dale, 13 January 1999.

12 Confusingly, Muuntux was also the name of Wong's ready-to-wear line at the time, which existed independently of the boutique.

13 This describes the second Union Square store; Obiko moved from 540 Sutter Street to its final location at 794 Sutter Street in 1981.

14 Jean Williams Cacicedo is one of several artists who have recalled that when they showed Sakata a work that moved her, she would literally shriek with excitement. Conversation with Cacicedo, 13 March 2004.

15 Maureen O. Sajbel, "Obiko: Tracking the Unique," *Women's Wear Daily* (New York: Fairchild, 20 April 1984) 16.

16 Conversation with Nancy Chappell, 27 March 2004.

17 The first art museum exhibition I have been able to document was *Art for Wearing* at the San Francisco Museum of Modern Art in 1979. It was followed by several others, including *Art Forms and the Body* at the Los Angeles County Museum of Art (1988, guest-curated by collector/dealer Susie Hollingsworth). Wearable art exhibitions during the 1980s were often at smaller museums and art centers in smaller cities, such as *Maximum Coverage* at the Kohler Art Center in Sheboygan, WI (1980); *Body Wraps* at the Redding Museum and Art Center in Redding, CA (1986); and *Finery* at North Carolina State University (1988).

18 The second of the two exhibitions subsequently toured East Asia under the auspices of the United States Information Agency, likely the first time American art to wear was seen there.

19 I am grateful to Jill Heppenheimer and Barbara Lanning of Santa Fe Weaving Gallery for helping crystallize my thoughts on this issue.

20 Conversation with Marian Clayden, 6 May 1996.

21 Aimone, *The Fiberarts Book of Wearable Art*, 51.

22 Jo Ann C. Stabb, "The Wearable Movement: A Critical Look at the State of the Art," *Surface Design Journal* (Oakland, CA: Vol. 13, No. 1, Fall 1988) 29–31.

23 Although Atelier began with a wearable art focus, it has broadened to include small-scale fashion, artisan, and avant-garde collections.

24 Weltge, *Women's Work*, 167.

25 Susan Summa has commented that, currently, artwear is being copied by mass retailers like Chico's. Letter to the author, 12 July 2004.

26 Worth went so far as to adopt an "artistic" temperament and have himself portrayed, artistically dressed, striking a Rembrandt-like pose.

27 Leventon, "Using Art in Pursuit of Fashion," in Jiminez, ed., *Picturing French Style*, 19–20.

28 Amy Fine Collins, "Sequined Simulacra," *Art in America* (July 1988) 51–53.

29 "Wearable Art," *Harper's Bazaar* (March 1986) 300–303.

30 "Fashion for Art's Sake," *Vogue* (February 1997) 120–122.

31 See Stroud, ed., *An Industrious Art* for a fuller discussion of the artist-in-residence program at The Fabric Workshop.

32 Shibori here is used in its current meaning as a general term for shaped-resist-dyeing.

33 Wada, *Memory on Cloth*, 85–88.

34 Ibid., 112–120.

35 Teufel, *Koos Couture Collage*, 11.

36 Surprisingly, van den Akker accepted an invitation from the Bernina Fashion Show to participate in the 2004 competition.

37 Wada, *Memory on Cloth*, 113–115.

38 See Cathy Horyn, "Is Copying Really a Part of the Creative Process?," *New York Times* (9 April 2002).

39 Sameer Reddy, *Hintmag* (August 2003).

Chapter 3

1 Nancy A. Corwin, "The Kimono in American Art and Fashion, 1953–1996," in Stevens and Wada, eds., *The Kimono Inspiration*, 64.

2 Brandon, *Country Textiles of Japan*, 9.

3 Corwin, in *The Kimono Inspiration*, 64.

4 Dale, "The Kimono in the Art to Wear Movement," in *The Kimono Inspiration*, 103–104.

5 Conversation with Marian Clayden, 6 May 1996.

6 Conversation with Tim Harding, 23 February 1999.

7 Knitting machines were not unknown in wearable art earlier, however; Marika Contompasis was using a very basic one as early as 1972. See plate 3.14.

8 Now in the collection of the Oakland Museum of California.

9 Aimone, *The Fiberarts Book of Wearable Art*, 51. Smith's early career was spent as a production dyer making scarves, wall hangings, and fabric for fashion designers, and he has developed shibori methods that allow him to process unusually large quantities of cloth very quickly.

10 Schapiro, *Femmages*, 2.

11 Dale, *Art to Wear*, 8.

12 Ibid., 94–95.

13 *Maximum Coverage*, 25. Cope noted that the artist Peter Collingwood reacted to the shirt by sending her a fictitious description of trying to borrow a size 38 "shirt of poems" from the public library and discovering that all copies in that size were already in use.

14 Conversation with Frances Butler, 19 April 2004.

Chapter 4

1 Conversation with Jo Ann Stabb, 9 August 1999. Stabb recalls their activities as being generally well received and fairly influential, but acknowledged that some of the ceramists and glass artists were less than enchanted.

2 Chunghie Lee, letter to the author, 13 April 2004.

3 A 1977 British/American exchange program organized by the American Crafts Council and the British Crafts Centre International Committee allowed four craftspeople to spend a month in each other's country; two of the participants, the American Jody Klein and the Briton John Hinchcliffe, commented on the perceived divisions between the crafts and fine arts, the absence of crafts and art programs in British institutions with an academic focus, and the different focuses on technical accomplishment and creativity. See John Hinchcliffe and Jody Klein, "All Abroad!," *Crafts* (January/February 1978) 9–10.

4 Susie Freeman, for instance, in talking about the evolution of her work commented that in her early career she was more comfortable keeping her work within the British definition of crafts and looking to the Crafts Council, rather than the Arts Council, for support. Letter to the author, 3 May 2004.

5 Angela Wigglesworth, "Museums Collect," *Crafts* (September/October 1980) 17–18. This may be because fashion is considered, at least by some, to be a craft. Wigglesworth cites a 1980 survey of several British museums collecting contemporary crafts that named fashion as one of the collected crafts.

6 Geraldine Rudge, "Baubles, Bangles & Bustiers," *Crafts* (May/June 1991) 31–33.

7 By 1996, though still creating clothing, Cramp and Harley had left the group and Bertram-Brown and Corben were beginning to move into other areas of design, including music video direction. Today, the New RenaisCAnce is a top British design firm but clothing has ceased to be its focus.

8 Freeman's *Pharmacopoeia* garments are wearable, but they are not intended for streetwear. Freeman also makes wearable art with this same trademark fabric that is intended for streetwear, which she sells through galleries such as Julie: Artisans' Gallery in New York.

9 Larsen, ed., *Crosscurrents*, 35.

10 Tomlinson, *Jewelry: Means: Meaning*, 51.

11 Betsky, *A Modern Movement*, 3.

12 There are also feltmakers elsewhere in Europe, in the United States, and in Japan.

13 Thomas, ed., *Filz*, 66–75.

14 The process of fulling, whereby fibers are matted together to create felt, involves wetting the fibers, rolling them up, and working them by beating or walking on them. See Ibid., 64–65.

15 Wada, *Memory on Cloth*, 44–45. The World Shibori Network sponsors frequent international conferences in far-flung places that have included Ahmedabad, Santiago, Melbourne, and Harrogate.

16 Ibid., 73.

17 Although Galerie Smend's artists are primarily German, it has shown work by artists from other European countries, Asia, and the United States. Galerie Smend also continues to show antique and contemporary batik from both Indonesia and Europe.

18 The 2003 winner was awarded 2,000 Euros; second place received 1,000, and third place received 500.

19 Cochrane, *The Crafts Movement in Australia*, 221.

20 In 2004 the show was slated for seven performances plus a public dress rehearsal, with a potential total audience of 20,000.

21 In 2004 a total of NZ $95,000 was available to be awarded.

22 Douglas Bullis, *Fashion Asia*, 68.

23 According to Chunghie Lee, there was a decline in interest in artwear in Korea at the end of the 1990s. Conversation with Lee, October 2003.

24 See, for example, Bae Chun Bun's introduction to *Fashion Art from Korea*, 11, and Jae-won Park's introduction to the *Kwangju Biennale International Art to Wear* exhibition catalogue (Kwangju, Korea, 1995) 8.

25 This aspect of wearable art in Korea was suggested by Chunghie Lee, who has taught at Hongik University. Conversation with Lee, 6 June 2004.

26 The use of *pojagi* by Lee and other Korean artists has interested artists in other parts of the world, and *pojagi* is now being explored by European and American artists as well.

27 Conversation with Jo Ann Stabb, 9 August 1999.

28 See Itchiku Kubota, *Opulence*.

Chapter 5

1 See Goldberg, *Performance Art*, 177–181.

2 For a chronicle of the development of the fashion show and its relationship to performance art, see Caroline Evans, "The Enchanted Spectacle," *Fashion Theory*, 271–310.

3 Recently, Cave began to create *Sound Suits* that make no sound; they are completely embellished with beads and sequins, and through them he is exploring the idea that sound can be identified with color, repeating pattern, and the reflection of light.

4 Catherine Morris and Dara Meyers-Kingsley, "Off the Wall: The Development of Robert Kushner's Fashion and Performance Art, 1970–76," *Fashion Theory*, 315–317. Several members of Kushner's family were in the clothing business and, unusually for a male, he was taught by his grandmother to crochet when he was seven. His interest in exploring gender issues through textiles and clothing was sparked by the negative reactions he experienced when, as a college student, he took up crochet seriously.

5 Ibid., 313.

6 *Clothing, Constructed and Eaten*, which took place in Los Angeles earlier in 1972, was an earlier version of *Robert Kushner and Friends Eat Their Clothes*. *The Art Rite Fashion Show* (1974) was a six-costume performance staged at the request of the journal *Art Rite* for a cocktail party benefit. Twenty years later, in October 1994, Kushner made his last edible performance costume for the Dada Ball in New York, a pumpkin bra and buttock cover worn with a mini-skirt of collard greens. For a detailed account of Kushner's work with edible costume, see Kushner, "Food + Clothing =," *Gastronomica*, 77–85.

7 Conversation with Robert Kushner, 11 July 2002.

8 Robert Kushner, "The Persian Line," *Eddy: About Dance* (No. 10, Summer 1978) quoted in Morris and Meyers-Kingsley, *Fashion Theory*, 327.

9 Charles Talley, "Pat Oleszko: Mastering the Visual Pun," *Surface Design Journal* (Vol. 14, No. 3, Spring 1990) 18.

10 Ibid., 16. *New Yuck Woman* was an unusual museum exhibition: the costumes were hung in the museum but every day Oleszko would don one of them and walk around the city in that character.

11 Terri Lonnier, "Altered Ego," *Fiberarts* (Vol. 10, No. 1, January/February 1983) 28.

12 Hollander, *Seeing Through Clothes*, xv.

13 Barbara Ward Grubb, "Finery: The Curator's Perspective," in *Finery*, 21.

14 Dale, "The Kimono in the Art to Wear Movement," in *The Kimono Inspiration*, 109.

15 Interestingly, similar ideas of presence/absence and memory were explored in a related way by American artist Jan Janeiro in a series of garments made in the 1970s. See Stevens and Wada, eds., *The Kimono Inspiration*, 103.

16 Schoettle, who returned to the United States in the 1990s after living in Europe for eleven consecutive years, makes artwear under the label Mau.

17 Kangas, *Jean Williams Cacicedo*, 9.

18 *Femmages* is a term coined by Schapiro as a sister of or alternative to terms like collage, assemblage, and découpage to denote those activities specifically as they were and are "practiced by women using traditional women's techniques to achieve their art—sewing, piecing, hooking, cutting, appliquéing, cooking and the like—activities also engaged in by men but assigned in history to women." See Schapiro, *Femmages*, 2.

19 Miller, *Figuratively Speaking*, 10. When Shea moved on to three-dimensional sculpture in the late 1970s she continued to make garments, first from wire mesh and sheet metal and later cast in bronze from a felt prototype, which she presents as archetypal male and female forms. While they are not fashionable in an up-to-the-minute sense (the male archetype is a rumpled overcoat, the female a form-fitting sleeveless sheath), they actually reference the adult fashions of Shea's childhood.

20 Dutch Wax cloth, which was first produced in the late nineteenth century, is a relatively recent development in this sort of cross-cultural textile pollination, which, as textile historians are well aware, has been going on for centuries. Judging from the press Shonibare has received over the past decade, however, it is news to the art world.

21 Golbin, *Fashion Designers*, 123.

Bibliography

Aimone, Katherine Duncan. *The Fiberarts Book of Wearable Art.* Asheville, NC: Lark Books, 2002.

Anscombe, Isabelle. *Omega and After: Bloomsbury and the Decorative Arts.* London: Thames & Hudson, 1981.

Artwear: The Body Adorned. Video, 55 min. San Francisco: KQED, 1990.

Ayres, Dianne, Timothy Hansen, Beth Ann McPherson, and Tommy Arthur McPherson II. *American Arts and Crafts Textiles.* New York: Harry N. Abrams, 2002.

Betsky, Aaron. *A Modern Movement: The Work of Maria Blaisse.* Perth, Australia: Perth Institute of Contemporary Art, 2004.

Blum, Dilys E. *Ahead of Fashion: Hats of the 20th Century.* Philadelphia: Philadelphia Museum of Art, 1993.

Bolz, Diane M. "Itchiku Kubota's Fascination with an Ancient Textile." *Smithsonian Magazine*, December 1995.

Bowman, Leslie Greene. *American Arts & Crafts: Virtue in Design.* Los Angeles: Los Angeles County Museum of Art, 1990.

Brandon, Reiko Mochinaga. *Country Textiles of Japan.* New York: John Weatherhill, 1986.

Breuer, Karin, Ruth E. Fine, and Steven A. Nash. *Thirty-Five Years at Crown Point Press.* Berkeley: The University of California Press, 1997.

Brown, Alix, and Anne Bissonnette. *Toledo Toledo.* New York: Visionaire Publishing, 2000.

Bullis, Douglas, ed. *California Fashion Designers.* Layton, Utah: Gibbs M. Smith, 1987.

——————. *Fashion Asia.* London and New York: Thames & Hudson, 2000.

Burnham, Dorothy K. *Cut My Cote.* Toronto: Royal Ontario Museum, 1973.

Calloway, Stephen, ed. *Liberty of London: Masters of Style and Decoration.* Boston: Little, Brown/The House of Liberty, London: Thames & Hudson, 1992.

Cochrane, Grace. *The Crafts Movement in Australia: A History.* Kensington, NSW: New South Wales University Press, 1992.

Coleman, Elizabeth Ann. *The Opulent Era: Fashions of Worth, Doucet, and Pingat.* London and New York: The Brooklyn Museum/Thames & Hudson, 1989.

Constantine, Mildred, and Jack Lenor Larsen. *Beyond Craft: The*

Art Fabric. New York: Van Nostrand Reinhold, 1972.

Cook, Robert. "Fashion: Between Containment and Chaos." www.realtimearts.net: RealTime, 2004.

Cunningham, Patricia. *Reforming Fashion, 1850–1914: Politics, Health, and Art.* Columbus, OH: Ohio State University, 2000.

_____. *Reforming Women's Fashion, 1850–1920: Politics, Health and Art.* Kent, OH: Kent State University Press, 2003.

Dale, Julie Schafler. *Art to Wear.* New York: Abbeville Press, 1986.

Damase, Jacques. *Sonia Delaunay: Fashion and Fabrics.* London: Thames & Hudson and New York: Harry N. Abrams, 1991.

De Osma, Guillermo. *Fortuny.* New York: Rizzoli and London: Aurum Press, 1980.

De Teliga, Jane. *Australian Fashion: The Contemporary Art.* Sydney: Museum of Applied Arts and Sciences, 1989.

Fashion Art from Korea: Air of the East. Seoul: Korea Fashion & Culture Association, 2000.

Fashion Theory: Fashion and Performance Special Issue. Oxford: Berg Publishers, Vol. 5, No. 3, September 2001.

Feldman, Del Pitt. *Crochet: Discovery and Design.* Garden City, NY: Doubleday, 1972.

Felshin, Nina. *Empty Dress: Clothing as Surrogate in Recent Art.* New York: Independent Curators, 1993.

Finery. Raleigh, NC: North Carolina State University, 1988.

Golbin, Pamela. *Fashion Designers.* New York: Watson-Guptill, 2001.

Goldberg, RoseLee. *Performance Art from Futurism to the Present,* rev. ed. London and New York: Thames & Hudson, 2001.

Hall, Marian, Marjorie Carne, and Sylvia Sheppard. *California Fashion from the Old West to New Hollywood.* New York: Harry N. Abrams, 2002.

Harlow, Eve. *The Jeans Scene.* New York: Drake Publishers, 1973.

Harris, Jane. "Beauty in the Beast." Pixel Raiders, 1993.

Hickey, Dave. "The Art Guys Get Legit." *Suits: The Clothes Make The Man.* New York: Harry N. Abrams, 2000.

Holborn, Mark. *Issey Miyake.* Cologne: Taschen, 1995.

Hollander, Anne. *Seeing Through Clothes.* New York: Viking Press, 1978.

_____. *Sex and Suits.* New York: Knopf, 1994.

Jacopetti, Alexandra. *Native Funk & Flash.* San Francisco: Scrimshaw Press, 1974.

Jewelry International. New York: American Craft Museum, 1984.

Jewelry USA. New York: American Craft Museum, 1984.

Johnson, Pamela. *Bodyscape: Caroline Broadhead.* Nottingham: Angel Row Gallery, 1999.

Kamitsis, Lydia. *Fashion Memoir: Paco Rabanne.* London: Thames & Hudson, 1999.

Kangas, Matthew. *Jean Williams Cacicedo: Explorations in Cloth.* San Francisco: Museum of Craft and Folk Art, 2002.

Kirke, Betty. *Madeleine Vionnet.* San Francisco: Chronicle Books, 1998.

Koide, Yokiko, Yoshinori Kamo, and Tomoko Furui, trans. *Nui Project: Embroidery Stitches.* Kagashima City, Japan: Shobu Gakuen, 2003.

Kubota, Itchiku. Tomoyuki Yamanobe, ed. *Opulence: The Kimonos and Robes of Itchiku Kubota.* Tokyo and New York: Kodansha International, 1984.

Kushner, Robert. "Food + Clothing =," *Gastronomica.* Berkeley: University of California, Vol. 4, No. 1, Winter 2004.

_____, Ed Friedman, and Katherine Landman. *The New York Hat Line.* New York: Bozeaux of London Press, 1979.

Larsen, Helge, ed. *Crosscurrents.* Sydney: Powerhouse Museum, 1984.

Larsen, Jack Lenor, Alfred Bühler, and Bronwen and Garrett Solyom. *The Dyer's Art: Ikat, Batik, Plangi.* New York: Van Nostrand Reinhold, 1976.

Leonard, Polly. "Ideas Become Objects: Anda Klancic's Machine-Embroidered Lace." *Embroidery,* Vol. 53, No. 1.

Leventon, Melissa. "Art to Wear." *The Fabric of Life: 150 Years of*

Northern California Fiber Art History. San Francisco: San Francisco State University, 1997.

_____. "Using Art in Pursuit of Fashion." *Picturing French Style: Three Hundred Years of Art and Fashion.* Mobile, AL: Mobile Museum of Art, 2003.

Levi's Denim Art Contest Catalogue of Winners. Mill Valley, CA: Baron Wolman/Squarebooks in conjunction with Owens, 1974.

Lewis, Linda. "Rags." *The Seattle Post-Intelligencer.* Seattle, WA: 1 May 1977.

Lineberry, Heather Sealy. *Art on the Edge of Fashion.* Tempe, AZ: Arizona State University Art Museum, 1997.

Loebenthal, Joel. *Radical Rags: Fashions of the Sixties.* New York: Abbeville Press, 1990.

McCarty, Cara, and Matilda McQuaid. *Structure and Surface: Contemporary Japanese Textiles.* New York: Museum of Modern Art, 1998.

Mangan, Kathleen Nugent. *Art to Wear: New American Handmade Clothing.* New York: American Craft Museum, 1984.

_____. *Art to Wear: New Handmade Clothing.* New York: American Craft Museum, 1983.

Marshall, John. *Make Your Own Japanese Clothes.* New York: Kodansha America, 1988.

Martin, Richard. *Universe of Fashion: Versace.* New York: Universe Publishing/Vendome Press, 1997.

Maximum Coverage: Wearables by Contemporary American Artists. Sheboygan, WI: John Michael Kohler Arts Center, 1980.

Mazza, Samuele. *Brahaus.* Milan: Idea Books, 1992.

_____. *Cinderella's Revenge.* San Francisco: Chronicle Books, 1994.

_____. *In the Bag.* San Francisco: Chronicle Books, 1997.

Miller, Nancy. *Figuratively Speaking: Drawings By Seven Artists.* Purchase, NY: Neuberger Museum, 1989.

Milinaire, Catherine, and Carol Troy. *Cheap Chic Update.* New York: Harmony Books, 1978.

Mode et Art, 1960–1990. Brussels: Société des Expositions du Palais des Beaux-Arts, 1995.

Morano, Elizabeth. *Sonia Delaunay: Art Into Fashion.* New York: George Braziller, 1986.

Newton, Stella Mary. *Health, Art, and Reason.* London: John Murray, 1974.

O'Connor, Naomi, *Wearable Art: Design for the Body.* Nelson, NZ: Craig Potton Publishing, 1996.

Owens, Richard M., Tony Lane, Peter Beagle, and Baron Wolman. *American Denim: A New Folk Art.* New York: Harry N. Abrams, 1975.

Parry, Linda, ed. *William Morris.* London: Philip Wilson/Victoria & Albert Museum, 1996.

Rathbun, William Jay, ed. *Beyond the Tanabata Bridge: Traditional Japanese Textiles.* New York: Seattle Art Museum/Thames & Hudson, 1993.

Rhodes, Zandra, and Anne Knight. *The Art of Zandra Rhodes.* Boston: Houghton Mifflin, 1985.

Riddell, Mary. "Interview With Fashion Designer Helen Storey." *New Statesman.* London: 12 September 1997.

Saint Laurent, Yves, et al. *Yves Saint Laurent.* New York: Metropolitan Museum of Art, 1983.

Schapiro, Miriam. *Art: A Woman's Sensibility.* Valencia, CA: California Institute of the Arts, 1975.

_____. *Femmages, 1971–1985.* St. Louis, MO: Brentwood Gallery, 1985.

_____. Interview by Ruth Bowman, East Hampton, NY, 10 September 1989. Archives of American Art, Smithsonian Institution.

Schweiger, Werner J. *Wiener Werkstätte: Design in Vienna 1903–1932.* London: Thames & Hudson and New York: Abbeville Press, 1984.

The 6th International Textile Competition '99. Kyoto: International Textile Fair Executive Committee, 1999.

Smend, Rudolf. *Seidenmalerei in Vollendung.* Niedernhausen: Falken-Verlag, 1988.

_____. *25 Jahre Textile Kunst: Galerie Smend 1973–1998.* Cologne: Galerie Smend, 1988.

Smith, Beryl, Joan Arbeiter, and Sally Shearer Swensen. *Lives and Works: Talks With Women Artists.* Lanham, MD: The Scarecrow Press, Vol. 2, 1996.

Smith, Paul J. et al. *Body Covering.* New York: American Craftsmen's Council, 1968.

_____ et al. *Homage to the Bag.* New York: American Crafts Council, 1976.

_____. et al. *The Great American Foot.* New York: American Crafts Council, 1978.

_____ and Edward Lucie-Smith. *Craft Today: The Poetry of the Physical.* New York: American Craft Museum/Weidenfeld & Nicolson, 1986.

Smith, Ronn. "All The World's a Stooge." *Theatre Crafts,* October 1980, 21–68.

Spiller, Eric. *New Departures in British Jewellery.* London: Crafts Council, 1983.

Stevens, Rebecca A.T., and Yoshiko Iwamoto Wada, eds. *The Kimono Inspiration: Art and Art-to-Wear in America.* San Francisco: Pomegranate Artbooks, 1996.

Stroud, Marion Bolton, et al. *A Decade of Pattern: Prints, Pieces and Prototypes from the Fabric Workshop.* Philadelphia: the Fabric Workshop, 1987.

_____, ed. *An Industrious Art: Innovation in Pattern and Print at the Fabric Workshop.* New York: W.W. Norton, 1991.

Sunset Ideas for Clothing Decoration. Menlo Park, CA: Lane Publishing, 1977.

Teufel, Linda Chang. *Koos Couture Collage Inspiration & Techniques.* Worthington, OH: Dragon Threads, 2002.

Thomas, Katharina, ed. *Filz: Kunst, Kunsthandwerk und Design.* Stuttgart: Arnoldsche Art Publishers, 2000.

Tilke, Max. *Costume Patterns and Designs.* London: A. Zwemmer, 1956.

Tomlinson, Michael. *Jewelry: Means: Meaning.* Knoxville, TN: The University of Tennessee, 1989.

Volcker, Angela. *Textiles of the Wiener Werkstätte 1912–1932.* New York: Rizzoli, 1994.

Wada, Yoshiko Iwamoto. *Memory on Cloth: Shibori Now.* New York: Kodansha America, 2002.

_____, Mary Kellogg Rice, and Jane Barton. *Shibori: The Inventive Art of Japanese Shaped Resist Dyeing: Tradition, Techniques, Innovation.* New York: Kodansha International, 1983.

Weiss, Wendy, Michael James, and Ana Lisa Hedstrom. *Process=Pattern: The Hand-dyed and Digitally Printed Textiles of Ana Lisa Hedstrom.* Lincoln, NE: The Robert Hillestad Textiles Gallery, 2004.

Weissmann, David, and Bill Weber, *The Cockettes.* 35mm, 100 min. GranDelusion Productions, San Francisco, 2002.

Weltge, Sigrid Wortmann. *Women's Work: Textile Art from the Bauhaus.* San Francisco: Chronicle Books, 1993.

Wendt, Selene. *Art Through the Eye of a Needle.* Høvikodden, Norway: Henie Onstad Kunstsenter, 2000.

White, Nicola. *Versace.* London: Carlton Books, 1999.

Wilcox, Claire. *Radical Fashion.* London: Victoria & Albert Museum, 2001.

Wolman, Baron. *Classic Rock & Other Rollers.* Santa Rosa, CA: Squarebooks, 1992.

Wollen, Peter, et al. *Addressing the Century: 100 Years of Art & Fashion.* London: Hayward Gallery Publishing, 1998.

Periodicals: *American Craft; Crafts; Fiberarts; Harper's Bazaar; Ornament; Surface Design Journal; Threads; Vogue.*

Exhibition Checklist

1 Phoebe Adams, American (b. 1953), created in collaboration with the Fabric Workshop and Museum, Philadelphia
Vice Master (jacket), 1987
Shell: pigment on silk dupioni; lining: pigment on silk satin
The Fabric Workshop and Museum

2 Estelle Akamine, American (b. 1954)
Red and Black Cocktail Dress, 1984
Dress: screen, grommets, exterior enamel paint; hat: screen, rattan
Collection of Donna Bellorado

3 Alex and Lee, American (active 1970–present)
Marilyn Necklace, 1972
Mixed media
Collection of Lee Brooks and Greg Franke

4 Alex and Lee, American (active 1970–present)
Chrysalis Necklace, 1973
Mixed media
Collection of Lee Brooks and Greg Franke

5 Diana Aurigemma, American (b. 1946)
Portable Culture Coat and Carrying Case, 1978, from Friends of the Rag, *Traveling Modes and Devices*
Mixed media
Collection of the artist

6 Patricia Black, Australian (b. 1956)
The Luminous Bardo, 1995
Silk; *itajime* shibori-dyed
Collection of World of Wearable Art Museum, Nelson, New Zealand

7 Gaza Bowen, American (1944–2005)
The American Dream, 1990, from the *Shoes for the Little Woman* series
Sponge, clothespins, kidskin, neoprene, pressboard, Astroturf, found objects
Fine Arts Museums of San Francisco, museum purchase, gift of the Textile Arts Council

8 Gaza Bowen, American (1944–2005)
K. Lee, You're On Your Own, 1983
Kidskin, lizard, leather, wine corks, rubber
Private collection

9 Gaza Bowen, American (1944–2005)
The Little Woman's Night Out, 1987, from the *Shoes for the Little Woman* series
Copper and stainless steel scrubbies, brass brushes and washers, Kopper Kloth®, wood, sink drains
Fine Arts Museums of San Francisco, museum purchase, Barbara Donohoe Jostes Bequest Fund

10 Reina Mia Brill, American (b. 1971)
First Steps, 1999
Hand-knitted coated copper wire
Collection of the artist

11 Walter Brix, German (b. 1965)
Hitoe Hosonaga (unlined kimono), 1998
Stiffened viscose, cotton, Chinese ink; calligraphy
Collection of the artist

12 Caroline Broadhead, British (b. 1950)
Sleeve, 1981
Nylon monofilament; dyed and woven
Museum of Arts and Design, New York, gift of Donna Schneier
1997.6.6

13 Caroline Broadhead, British (b. 1950)
Wraparound Shirt, 1983
Cotton
Collection of the artist

14 Frances Butler, American (b. 1940)
New Dryads Dress, 1979
Letterpress-printed organdy, letterpress-printed and hand-colored paper
Collection of the artist

15 Jean Williams Cacicedo, American (b. 1948)
Pink Petals, 1978
Hand- and loom-knitted wool; dyed, pieced, appliquéd
Fine Arts Museums of San Francisco, gift of Bunny Horowitz
1992.161

16 Jean Williams Cacicedo, American (b. 1948)
Rain Coat: San Francisco Bay, 1999
Wool knit; fulled, dyed, slashed, pieced
Collection of Sylvia Elsesser

17 Thea Cadabra, British (b. 1951), and James Rooke, British (b. 1945)
Maid Shoe, 1982
Mixed media
Fine Arts Museums of San Francisco, gift of Diane K. Lloyd-Butler 114.2a–b

18 Thea Cadabra, British (b. 1951), and James Rooke, British (b. 1945)
Palm Tree Sandals, 1982
Mixed media
Fine Arts Museums of San Francisco, gift of Diane K. Lloyd-Butler 114.2a–b

19 Nick Cave, American (b. 1959)
Sound Suit, 2004
Found beaded and sequined garments; de- and reconstructed
Collection of the artist

20 Nancy Chappell, American (b. 1938)
Dragon Dress, 1995
Silk, satin, and silk and metal organza, couched gold thread embroidery, tassels
Collection of Nancy Ung

21 Nancy Chappell, American (b. 1938)
Kabuki Opera Coat, 1985
Painted cotton
Philadelphia Museum of Art, gift of Theodore E. Yaeger III in memory of Joyce Brady Yaeger

22 Cat Chow, American (b. 1973)
Not For Sale, 2002
Currency, fishing line, glue
Collection of the artist

23 Marian Clayden, working in the U.S. (b. U.K., 1937)
Viennese Bias Dress, 1995
Silk devoré velvet; resist-dyed and discharged
Fine Arts Museums of San Francisco, gift of the artist
1996.32a–c

24 Ben Compton, American (1938–1986), and Marian Clayden, working in the U.S. (b. U.K., 1937)
Nocturnal Moth, 1974
Silk super organza, steel corset stays, nylon "horsehair" braids, silk veiling, cotton lace, elasticized harness; dyed, clamped, discharged, dipped, burned, cut, pieced, stitched
Courtesy of Marian Clayden and Julie Schafler Dale, Custodian, Estate of Ben Compton

25 Judith Content, American (b. 1957)
Sweltering Sky, 1992
Thai silk; *arashi* shibori-dyed and discharged, pieced, quilted, and appliquéd
Fine Arts Museums of San Francisco, museum purchase, Textile Arts Council Endowment Fund and Judith Content
2001.130

26 Marika Contompasis, American (b. 1948)
Wedding Ensemble, 1972
Loom-knitted and crocheted hand-dyed wool; embroidery
Collection of Jeanne Rose #4

27 Louise Todd Cope, American (b. 1930), created in collaboration with the Fabric Workshop and Museum, Philadelphia
Poetry Shirt, 1978
Silkscreen on linen
Collection of the Fabric Workshop and Museum

28 Louise Todd Cope, American (b. 1930)
Masada Jacket, late 1960s
Wool; handwoven
Philadelphia Museum of Art, gift of Helen Williams Drutt English in honor of the artist, 2000
2000-142-1

29 Randall Darwall, American (b. 1947)
Shawls and Scarves, 1980s–1990s
Silk; dyed, handwoven
Collection of Peggy Taylor

30 Randall Darwall, American (b. 1947)
Scarves, 1980s–1990s
Silk; dyed, handwoven
Collection of Tam Martinides Gray

31 Designer Unknown, American
Aesthetic Evening Dress, ca. 1895–1900
Eggplant wool challis and pink and blue shot silk taffeta
Fine Arts Museums of San Francisco, gift of Mrs. Marie Doran
59.48.13

32 Lam de Wolf, Dutch (b. 1949)
Headdress, 1984
Textile, wood, paint
The Museum of Fine Arts, Houston; Helen Williams Drutt Collection
2002.3724

33 Lam de Wolf, Dutch (b. 1949)
Headdress #14, 1984
Textile, wood, paint
The Museum of Fine Arts, Houston; gift of Helen Williams Drutt English
2003.919

34 Genevieve Dion, working in the U.S. (b. Canada, 1963)
Mermaid Dress, 1999
Gunma silk; shibori scoured and dyed
Collection of the artist

35 Lea Ditson, American (b. 1950)
Ensemble, mid-1980s
Silk; dyed and pieced
Collection of the artist

36 Nicki Hitz Edson, American (b. 1941)
First Mask, ca. 1969
Crocheted wool
Collection of Myrna Tatar

37 Nicki Hitz Edson, American (b. 1941)
Seascape Kimono, 1987
Loom-knitted wool
Collection of the artist. Courtesy of Julie: Artisans' Gallery

38 Del Pitt Feldman, American
Dress, ca. 1971
Crocheted rayon ribbon, cordé and twist cordé, mirrors, beads
Collection of Myrna Tatar

39 Arline Fisch, American (b. 1931)
Helen's Hat, 1985
Loom-knitted coated copper wire, silver accents
Museum of Fine Arts, Houston, Helen Williams Drutt Collection
2002.3743.1

40 Susie Freeman, British (b. 1956), and Dr. Liz Lee, British (b. 1955)
Come Dancing, 1998
Nylon, birth control pills; loom-knitted
Collection of the artists

41 Mariano Fortuny, Spanish, working in Italy (1874–1949)
Delphos and Belt, ca. 1930
Dyed pleated silk satin
Fine Arts Museums of San Francisco, gift of Barbara D. Jostes
78.56.46a–b

42 Mariano Fortuny, Spanish, working in Italy (1874–1949)
Evening Coat, ca. 1930
Stencil-printed dyed silk velvet
Fine Arts Museums of San Francisco, gift of Mrs. James Caldwell in memory of Sara Bard Field Wood
74.16.3

43 Nicolas Ghesquière for Balenciaga, French (b. 1972)
Collage Vest, 2002
Mixed media
Private Collection

44 Ann Hamilton, American (b. 1956), created in collaboration with the Fabric Workshop and Museum, Philadelphia
Untitled (collar), 1993
Horsehair, linen, antique buttons; embroidered
Philadelphia Museum of Art, gift of Marion Boulton Stroud, 1998
1998-167-1

45 Tim Harding, American (b. 1950)
Oaks, 1988
Cotton, free-reverse appliqué (collage-layered, quilted, slashed, frayed)
Collection of Sara and David Lieberman

46 Tim Harding, American (b. 1950)
Shroud #5, 1992
Cotton; collage-layered, quilted, slashed, frayed
Collection of the artist

47 Jane Harris, British (b. 1965)
Dress, late 1980s
Silk and synthetic; shibori-constructed and dyed
Collection of the artist

48 Ellen Hauptli, American (b. 1949)
Evening Ensemble, ca. 1995
Pleated polyester jacquard
Collection of Renée Dreyfus

49 Sharron Hedges, American (b. 1948)
Desert Ikat, 1989
Loom-knitted wool and other fibers
Fine Arts Museums of San Francisco, gift of Wittenborn & Hollingsworth

50 Ana Lisa Hedstrom, American (b. 1943)
Fan Vest, 1982
Shibori-dyed silk
Fine Arts Museums of San Francisco, museum purchase, gift of Jane R. Lurie, the Embroiderers Guild, and funds from the Textile Arts Trust Fund
1998.226.1

51 Ana Lisa Hedstrom, American (b. 1943)
Poncho, 1996
Silk; pieced, shibori-dyed
Collection of the artist

52 Susanna Heron, British (b. 1949)
Ruff, 1983
Nylon dyed with five different blacks
Collection of the artist

53 Susanna Heron, British (b. 1949)
Wearable, 1982
Cotton jersey, steel; knotted
Museum of Arts and Design, New York, gift of Donna Schneier
1997.6.23

54 Julia Hill, working in the U.S. (b. Germany, 1947)
American Velvet, 1988
Painted silk velvet
Museum of Arts and Design, New York, gift of the artist
1993.44

55 Käthi Hoppler-Dinkel, Swiss (b. 1950)
Schritt-für-Schritt-Stiefel (Boots), 2000
Black valasian and merino wool; felted
Private collection

56 Thomas Horst, American (b. 1971)
Aflame, 2002
Wool; felted
Collection of the artist

57 Nina Vivian Huryn, American (b. 1952)
Flip-Top Vest, 1989
Mixed media
Collection of Judy Kenyon Burness

58 Yoko Ishigaki, Japanese (b. 1978)
Hand Cover, 1999
Silk; wax-dyed, embroidered
Collection of the artist

59 Diane Jacobs, American (b. 1966)
Untitled (Red Hat), 1998
Letterpress on paper
Fine Arts Museums of San Francisco, museum purchase, Barbara Donohoe Jostes Fund
1998.137

60 Alexandra Jacopetti, American (b. 1939)
Roland's Shirt, late 1960s
Cotton; embroidered
Oakland Museum of California, gift of Alexandra Jacopetti Hart
83.102.1

61 Jorie Johnson, working in Japan (b. U.S., 1954)
Catch a Falling Star, from the *Aurora Borealis* series, 2002
Wool, holographic and polyester fibers, novelty yarn, metallic fabric; felted
Collection of the artist

62 Judith and Lin, American
Day Dress/Skirt and Jacket, ca. 1971
Rayon challis; tie-dyed and batiked
Collection of Marna Clark

63 Jeannette Kastenberg, American (b. 1963)
The Abstract, 1992
Sequins, beads, silk chiffon
Museum of Arts and Design, New York, gift of the artist
1992.74.2

64 Rose Kelly, American (b. 1955)
Longjohns, 1987
Painted cotton
Collection of the artist

65 Kenneth D. King, American (b. 1958)
Lucifer's Handmaiden, 1993
Taffeta, velvet, feathers, and beads
Fine Arts Museums of San Francisco, gift of Kenneth D. King
1997.189

66 Candace Kling, American (b. 1948)
She Sells Sea Shells, 1988
Mixed media; molded, pleated, quilted, folded, pressed, sewn
Fine Arts Museums of San Francisco, museum purchase, gift of the Maggie Brosnan Memorial Fund
1996.73

67 Candace Kling, American (b. 1948)
Red Rainbow, 1981
Mixed media
Collection of Camille and Alex Cook

68 Fred E. Kling, American (b. 1944)
Dragon Skirt, ca. 1974
Painted cotton
Fine Arts Museums of San Francisco, gift of Dr. Wanda Corn
2001.158.1

69 Fred E. Kling, American (b. 1944)
Wedding Dress, 1972
Painted cotton
Collection of Marna Clark

70 Dina Knapp, American (b. 1947)
Mother-of-Pearl Kimono, 1975
Wool, wool jersey, pearl buttons; crocheted, quilted, appliquéd
Fine Arts Museums of San Francisco, gift of Mrs. John N. Rosekrans, Jr.
1992.147.1

71 Dina Knapp, American (b. 1947)
See It Like a Native, History Kimono #1, 1982

Cotton, polyester, plastic, paper; painted, appliquéd, Xerox-transferred, printed, assembled
Collection of the artist. Courtesy of Julie: Artisans' Gallery

72 Jane Kosminsky, American (b. 1949)
Lizard Wizard, 1985
Punched and laced leather
Fine Arts Museums of San Francisco, gift of Wittenborn & Hollingsworth

73 Ina Kozel, working in the U.S. (b. Lithuania, 1944)
Our Lady of Rather Deep Waters, 1985
Resist-painted silk, color Xerox transfer, painted expanding foam plastic
Collection of the artist

74 Ina Kozel, working in the U.S. (b. Lithuania, 1944)
Robe from the Red Sea, 1988
Silk, wax-resist painted
Collection of the artist

75 Charlotte Kruk n' Kempken, American (b. 1971)
Peach Nectar, 2002
Mixed media
Collection of the artist

76 Robert Kushner, American (b. 1949)
Jacket, 1982
Screenprinted silk charmeuse
Fine Arts Museums of San Francisco Crown Point Press Archive, gift of Crown Point Press
1993.51.364

77 Robert Kushner, American (b. 1949)
Gula Faranghi (French Roses) from *The Persian Line I*, 1975
Chiffon; discharged
Collection of the artist

78 Chunghie Lee, Korean (b. 1945)
Durumagi, ca. 2000
Paper, oriental ink; dyed, stitched and quilted, silkscreened
Museum of Arts and Design, New York, gift of Dorothy Lemelson
2001.63

79 Liberty & Co., Artistic and Historic Costume Studio, British
Day Dress, ca. 1903
Raw silk pongee; smocked and embroidered with silk
Los Angeles County Museum of Art, gift of the Fine Arts Gallery of San Diego
M.69.31

80 Janet Lipkin, American (b. 1948)
Ensemble, *African Mask*, 1970
Hand-spun and dyed crocheted wool, leather, wood
The Metropolitan Museum of Art, gift of Muriel Kallis Newman 2003
2003.79.13a–c

81 Janet Lipkin, American (b. 1948)
Flamingo, 1982
Loom-knitted, hand-dyed wool
Collection of Judy Kenyon Burness

82 Janet Lipkin, American (b. 1948)
Jester Coat, early 1970s
Wool; crocheted
Fine Arts Museums of San Francisco, gift of the artist
1999.139.1

83 Janet Lipkin, American (b. 1948)
Nudes Coat, 1992

Loom-knitted wool
Fine Arts Museums of San Francisco, museum purchase, gift of the Textile Arts Council Endowment Fund
1999.144a–b

84 Christine LoFaso, American (b. 1950)
Redress: Gestation Corset, 1992
Paper, mink fur, metal, catnip-stained lacing, text from "Dora/A Case Study of Hysteria" by Sigmund Freud
Private collection

85 Bert Long, American (b.1940), created in collaboration with the Fabric Workshop and Museum
Home Sweet Home Clan Costume, 1993
Pigment on cotton sateen; silk satin lining
The Fabric Workshop and Museum

86 K. Lee Manuel, American (1936–2003)
Conflicts/Contrasts, 1982
Painted leather and feathers, buttons
Fine Arts Museums of San Francisco, gift of K. Lee Manuel

87 K. Lee Manuel, American (1936–2003)
Dream of a Chinese Princess #1, 1990
Feathers, leather; painted, assembled
Collection of David and Erin Reese

88 K. Lee Manuel, American (1936–2003)
Maxi Dress, ca. 1968
Painted cotton
Fine Arts Museums of San Francisco, gift of Barbara Feigel
1990.57.1

89 John Marshall, American (b. 1955)
Phoenix, 1981
Japanese silk wedding jacquard; *tsutsugaki* (rice-paste resist)
Private collection

90 Linda Mendelson, American (b. 1940)
Although I Called Another, Abra Came, 1989
Wool; loom-knitted, hand crocheted
The Garry and Sylvia Bennett Collection. Courtesy of Julie: Artisans' Gallery

91 Linda Mendelson, American (b. 1940)
I Made My Song a Coat, 1976
Loom-knitted wool
Collection of The Metropolitan Museum of Art, gift of Linda Mendelson
1982.309a–b

92 Doug Miles, American
Levi's, 1974
Painted cotton
Levi Strauss & Co. Archives, San Francisco

93 Norma Minkowitz, American (b. 1937)
Formal Gardens Coat, 1985
Crocheted cotton, suede
Fine Arts Museums of San Francisco, museum purchase, Textile Arts Council Endowment Fund
1999.100.1

94 Norma Minkowitz, American (b. 1937)
Headdress II, 1975
Crocheted and painted cotton
Fine Arts Museums of San Francisco, gift of the artist
1999.100.3

95 Norma Minkowitz, American (b. 1937)
Sit on It, 1980
Crocheted and knitted cotton and wool; stuffed and stiffened
Fine Arts Museums of San Francisco, gift of the artist
1999.100.2

96 Issey Miyake, Japanese (b. 1938), and
Yasumasa Morimura, Japanese (b. 1951)
Pleats Please: Guest Artist #1, 1996
Polyester; pleated and printed
Los Angeles County Museum of Art
AC1999.104.2

97 Issey Miyake, Japanese (b. 1938), and
Tim Hawkinson, American (b. 1960)
Pleats Please: Guest Artist #3, 1998
Polyester; pleated and printed
Los Angeles County Museum of Art
AC1999.99.2

98 Carol Motty, American
Aztec Jewel, 1990
Silicone with iridescent powders on painted
silk chiffon
Museum of Arts and Design, New York, gift
of Peggy and David Ross
1992.99

99 Peggy Moulton, American
Tree of Life Jeans, 1974
Embroidered cotton
The Oakland Museum of California
84.144.1

100 Risë Nagin, American (b. 1950)
Road Goliaths, 1985
Silk, cotton, acetate, polyester, acrylic paint;
pieced, appliquéd and stained
Museum of Arts and Design, New York, gift
of the artist
1995.56

101 Teresa Nomura, American (b. 1951)
Keep Your Sunny Side Up, 1983
Appliquéd cotton chintz, bead embroidery
Collection of Libby Cooper

102 Pat Oleszko, American (b. 1947)
Coat of Arms, 1975
Mixed media
Collection of the artist

103 Justine Limpus Parish, American (b. 1951)
Nouveau Renaissance, 2001
Silk satin and organza; digital inkjet-
printed, block-printed, painted, shibori-
dyed and pleated
Collection of Justine Limpus Parish

104 Jeung-Hwa Park, working in the U.S.
(b. Korea)
Inspiration of Falling Woods, 2000
Merino wool, silk; knitted, felted, resist-dyed
Museum of Arts and Design, New York,
museum purchase with funds provided by
Collections Committee
2000.11

105 Jeung-Hwa Park, working in the U.S.
(b. Korea)
Deep, Dark Leaves, 1999
Merino wool, silk; knitted, felted, resist-dyed
Museum of Arts and Design, New York,
museum purchase with funds provided by
Collections Committee
2000.109

106 Jody Pinto, American (b. 1942), created in
collaboration with the Fabric Workshop
and Museum
Hair Shirt, 1978
Pigment on pigskin
Collection of the Fabric Workshop and
Museum

107 Yvonne Porcella, American (b. 1936)
Diamonds on Ice, 1984
Silk; painted, airbrushed, appliquéd, quilted

Fine Arts Museums of San Francisco, gift of
the artist
1994.161.4

108 Yvonne Porcella, American (b. 1936)
Pasha on the 10:04, 1984
Pieced, painted, and quilted cotton
Collection of the artist

109 Yvonne Porcella, American, (b. 1936)
Short Tunic with Mola Sleeve, ca. 1971
Cotton, mirror cloth, found objects
Fine Arts Museums of San Francisco, gift
of Yvonne B. Porcella in memory of
Margaret A. Brosnan
1994.161.2

110 Victoria Rabinowe, American (b. 1949), and
Ed Oppenheimer, American (b. 1947)
Tidepool Coat, 1989
Cotton, silk; woven, dyed, painted
Collection of the artists

111 Debra Rapoport, American (b. 1945)
Hoop Hat with Beaded Flowers, 1993
Nineteenth-century cage crinoline, vintage
beaded flowers, millinery foliage, tinsel
cording, metallic fabric
Philadelphia Museum of Art, gift of Helen
Williams Drutt English in honor of the
artist, 2000
2000-142-3

112 Jon Eric Riis, American (b. 1945)
Heart of Gold Female #2, 2002
Tapestry-woven silk and metallic thread
Collection of Deena and Jerry Kaplan

113 Mario Rivoli, American (b. 1943)
Mexican Jacket, 1989
Cotton, buttons, found objects; assemblage
Collection of Marsha Bohr

114 Jacquelyn Roesch-Sanchez, American
(b. 1946)
Dark Dream, 1988
Rayon; loom-knitted
Collection of the artist

115 Barbara Rogers, Australian (b. 1955)
African Notions, 1999
Silk georgette, kangaroo leather; shibori-
dyed and discharged
Collection of the artist

116 Galya Rosenfeld, American Israeli (b. 1977)
Pinafore 2, 2002
Cotton muslin, straight pins
Collection of the artist

117 Marian Schoettle, American (b. 1954)
Contour Couture, 2004
Rayon; embroidered
Collection of the artist

118 Carol Lee Shanks, American, (b. 1957)
Scarification Fairy (skirt, wrap, vest), 2001
Gunma silk; pieced, bundle-resisted, stitch-
resisted, scoured
Collection of the artist

119 Carol Lee Shanks, American, (b. 1957)
Ritual Tunic with Spine, 1997
Linen, banana fiber, plant pods, twigs;
assembled
Collection of the artist

120 Carter Smith, American (b. 1946)
Rainbow Delight, 2004
Silk; shibori-dyed
Collection of the artist

121 Mimi Smith, American (b. 1942)
Steel Wool Peignoir, 1966
Steel wool, nylon, lace
Spencer Museum of Art, University of
Kansas, museum purchase: Helen Foresman
Spencer Acquisition Fund
2000.17

122 Joan Steiner, American
Kitchen Vest, 1977
Velvet, cotton, rayon, satin, found objects
Philadelphia Museum of Art, gift of Mrs.
Robert L. McNeil Jr., 1994
1994-92-5

123 Helen Storey, British (b 1959)
Spinal Column Dress, 1997, from the
Primitive Streak Collection
Printed silk, silver foil, and fiber optics
The Helen Storey Foundation

124 Susan Summa, American (b. 1948)
*Life's More Fun When You Travel in a
Checker*, 1995
Loom-knitted wool
Collection of Myra Jennings

125 Deborah Valoma, American (b. 1955)
Following Ariadne's Thread, 1992
Rayon, cotton; woven, dip-dyed
Collection of the artist

126 Deborah Valoma, American (b. 1955)
Moment in Thebes, 1987
Wool; pieced and appliquéd
Collection of the artist

127 Yoshiko Wada, working in the U.S.
(b. Japan, 1945)
Coca-Cola Kimono, 1975
Linen; weft-ikat
Promised gift of the artist to the Fine Arts
Museums of San Francisco

128 Katherine Westphal, American (b. 1919)
Giverny II, 1983
Handmade paper, cotton, silk brocade,
color Xerox; dyed, stamped, pieced
Museum of Fine Arts, Boston, The Daphne
Farago Collection

129 Katherine Westphal, American (b. 1919)
Koi, 1985
Handmade paper, Lurex; dyed, transfer-
printed, painted, pieced
Museum of Fine Arts, Boston, The Daphne
Farago Collection

130 Katherine Westphal, American (b. 1919)
Poncho, 1970s
Printed panné velvet
From the collection of Cameron Silver

131 White Duck Workshop, American (active
1960s–1970s)
Maxi Dress, ca. 1970
Appliquéd cotton
Fine Arts Museums of San Francisco, gift of
Dr. Wanda Corn
2001.158.2

132 Fashion Studio of the Wiener Werkstätte,
Austrian (1910–31)
Woman's Afternoon Dress, ca. 1917
Silk chiffon, net, and embroidery
Los Angeles County Museum of Art,
Costume Council Fund
AC1999.178.1

133 Fashion Studio of the Wiener Werkstätte,
Austrian (1910–31)
Woman's Afternoon Dress, ca. 1917

Silk chiffon, net, and embroidery
Los Angeles County Museum of Art,
Costume Council Fund
AC1999.178.2

134 William T. Wiley, American (b. 1937)
Mr. and Mrs. Casual in Smoothasilk, 1982
Screenprinted silk charmeuse
Fine Arts Museums of San Francisco,
Crown Point Press Archive, gift of Crown
Point Press
1993.51.365a–b

135 Kaisik Wong, American (1950–1990)
Yellow/Green Ray, 1974, from *The Seven
Rays* series
Synthetic gauze, lamé, brocade; appliquéd
Fine Arts Museums of San Francisco,
museum purchase, gift of Alma Kay Wong,
the Textile Arts Council Endowment Fund,
Marian Clayden, Peggy Gordon, Pamela
Ransom, Santa Fe Weaving Gallery, Mr. and
Mrs. Alfred S. Wilsey, Susan York, and
various donors
1998.181.14a–b

136 Kaisik Wong, American (1950–1990)
Blue Ray, 1974, from *The Seven Rays* series
Synthetic gauze, lamé, brocade; appliquéd
Fine Arts Museums of San Francisco,
museum purchase, gift of Alma Kay Wong,
the Textile Arts Council Endowment Fund,
Marian Clayden, Peggy Gordon, Pamela
Ransom, Santa Fe Weaving Gallery, Mr. and
Mrs. Alfred S. Wilsey, Susan York, and
various donors
1998.181.16a–d

137 Kaisik Wong, American (1950–1990)
Collage Vest, ca. 1974
Mixed media
Collection of Kailey Wong

138 Kaisik Wong, American (1950–1990)
Orchid Dress, ca. 1976
Polyester jersey; airbrush-painted
Fine Arts Museums of San Francisco,
museum purchase, gift of Alma Kay Wong,
the Textile Arts Council Endowment Fund,
Marian Clayden, Peggy Gordon, Pamela
Ransom, Santa Fe Weaving Gallery, Mr. and
Mrs. Alfred S. Wilsey, Susan York,
and various donors
1998.181.5a–c

139 Kaisik Wong, American (1950–1990)
Self-Portrait as Monkey King, ca. 1980s
Gelatin silver print
Fine Arts Museums of San Francisco
Museum purchase, gift of Alma Kay Wong,
the Textile Arts Council Endowment Fund,
Marian Clayden, Peggy Gordon, Pamela
Ransom, Santa Fe Weaving Gallery, Mr. and
Mrs. Alfred S. Wilsey, Susan York, and
various donors
1998.181.25

140 Kansai Yamamoto, Japanese (b. 1944)
Kimono Dress, 1971
Wool and cotton ikat, leather, snakeskin;
appliquéd
Fine Arts Museums of San Francisco,
museum purchase, gift of the Textile Arts
Council Endowment Fund
1999.122

141 Rebekah Younger, American (b. 1955)
Patchwork Poncho II, 1999
Cotton and rayon; pieced, gradient-dyed
and discharged
Collection of Ruby Y. Peters

Credits

1.1 Fine Arts Museums of San Francisco, museum purchase, gift of the Textile Arts Council Endowment Fund. Photo: Joseph McDonald.
1.2 Courtesy of the estate of K. Lee Manuel. Photo: Barry Shapiro.
1.3 Los Angeles County Museum of Art, gift of the Fine Arts Gallery of San Diego. Photo: ©2001 Museum Associates, Los Angeles County Museum of Art. All Rights Reserved.
1.4 Courtesy of Randall Darwall. Photo: Morgan Rockhill.
1.5 Courtesy of Susie Hollingsworth. Photo: Tohru Nakamura.
1.6 Courtesy of Michiko Kawarabayashi. Photo: Hiroji Kawarabayashi.
1.7 Fine Arts Museums of San Francisco, museum purchase, gift of the artist. Photo courtesy of Yvonne Porcella; photography by Sharon Risedorph.
1.8 Fine Arts Museums of San Francisco, museum purchase, gift of Jane R. Lurie, the Embroiderers Guild, and funds from the Textile Arts Trust Fund. Photo: Joseph McDonald.
1.9 Fine Arts Museums of San Francisco, museum purchase, Textile Arts Council Endowment Fund and Judith Content. Photo: Joseph McDonald.
1.10 V&A Images/Victoria & Albert Museum.
1.11 Fine Arts Museums of San Francisco, gift of Mrs. Marie Doran. Photo: Joseph McDonald.
1.12 Los Angeles County Museum of Art, gift of the Fine Arts Gallery of San Diego. Photo: ©2001 Museum Associates, Los Angeles County Museum of Art. All Rights Reserved.
1.13 Originally published in *Das Kleid der Frau* (1904) by Alfred Mohrbutter.
1.14 Courtesy Historisches Museum der Stadt Wien.
1.15 Courtesy of Österreichische Nationalbibliothek. Photo: D'Ora.
1.16 Los Angeles County Museum of Art, Costume Council Fund. Photo: ©2001 Museum Associates, Los Angeles County Museum of Art. All Rights Reserved.
1.17 Fine Arts Museums of San Francisco, gift of Mrs. Alan Fleishhacker. Photo: Joseph McDonald.
1.18 Courtesy of Royal Ontario Museum.
1.19 Fine Arts Museums of San Francisco, museum purchase, gift of the Textile Arts Council Endowment Fund. Photo: Joseph McDonald.
1.20 Patrick Demarchelier/Courtesy of *Harper's Bazaar* .
1.21 Fine Arts Museums of San Francisco, gift of Mrs. John N. Rosekrans, Jr. Photo: Joseph McDonald.
1.22 Courtesy of Deborah Valoma. Photo: Lee Fatherree.
1.23 Fine Arts Museums of San Francisco, gift of Wittenborn & Hollingsworth. Photo: Joseph McDonald.
2.1 Courtesy of Baron Wolman. Photo: Baron Wolman.
2.2 Courtesy of The Museum of Arts and Design. Photo: Tohru Nakamura.
2.3 Fine Arts Museums of San Francisco. Tunic (right): The Eleanor Christenson de Guigné Collection (Mrs. Christian de Guigné III), gift of Ronna and Eric Hoffman. Tunic (left) and dress: gift of Barbara Feigel. Photo: Joseph McDonald.
2.4 Courtesy of Alexandra Hart and Ann Funston. Photo: Jerry Wainwright.
2.5 Fine Arts Museums of San Francisco, gift of Yvonne B. Porcella in memory of Margaret A. Brosnan. Photo: Joseph McDonald.
2.6 Courtesy of Fashion Institute of Design and Merchandising.
2.7 Courtesy of Bud Johns. Photo: Joseph McDonald.
2.8 Courtesy of Alexandra Hart and Ann Funston. Photo: Jerry Wainwright.
2.9 Courtesy of Doug Miles.
2.10 Courtesy of Peggy Moulton.
2.11 Fine Arts Museums of San Francisco, gift of Janet Lipkin. Photo: Joseph McDonald.
2.12 Courtesy of Myrna Tatar. Photo: Joseph McDonald.
2.13 Fine Arts Museums of San Francisco, museum purchase, gift of Alma Kay Wong, Textile Arts Council Endowment Fund, Marian Clayden, Peggy Gordon, Pamela Ransom, Santa Fe Weaving Gallery, Mr. and Mrs. Alfred S. Wilsey, Susan York, and various donors.
2.14 The Metropolitan Museum of Art, gift of Muriel Kallis Newman 2003. Photo: ©2004 The Metropolitan Museum of Art.
2.15 Fine Arts Museums of San Francisco, gift of Dr. Wanda Corn. Photo: Joseph McDonald.
2.16 Courtesy of Marna Clark and the Los Angeles County Museum of Art. Photo: © 2004 Museum Associates/LACMA.
2.17 Bill King/Courtesy of *Harper's Bazaar*.
2.18 Courtesy of Susie Hollingsworth. Photo: Tohru Nakamura.
2.19 Fine Arts Museums of San Francisco, gift of Dr. Wanda Corn. Photo: Joseph McDonald.
2.20 Courtesy of Ina Kozel.
2.21 Courtesy of Alma Kay Wong.
2.22 Courtesy of Lea Ditson.
2.23 Courtesy of Ana Lisa Hedstrom. Photo: Elaine Keenan.
2.24 Fine Arts Museums of San Francisco, gift of Janet Lipkin. Photo: Joseph McDonald.
2.25 Courtesy of Rebekah Younger. Photo: Chris Lawrence.
2.26 Fine Arts Museums of San Francisco, gift of the artist. Photo: Joseph McDonald.
2.27 Courtesy of Carter Smith. Photo: Joan Emm.
2.28 Courtesy of Candace Kling. Photo: John Bagley.
2.29 Courtesy of Lee Brooks and Greg Franke. Photo: Joseph McDonald.
2.30 Courtesy of Quilts, Inc. Photo: Perrault Studios.
2.31 Courtesy of Victoria Rabinowe. Photo: David Marlow.
2.32 Fine Arts Museums of San Francisco, gift of Janet Cooper. Photo: Joseph McDonald.
2.33 Courtesy of Yvonne Porcella. Photo: Sharon Risedorph.
2.34 As seen in *Art in America*, July 1988; photographer unknown.
2.35 Courtesy of Bill Blass, Ltd. Archives. Photo: Jesse Gerstein.
2.36 Art Kane/Courtesy of *Harper's Bazaar*
2.37 Courtesy of the Fabric Workshop and Museum Staff.
2.38 Fine Arts Museums of San Francisco, museum purchase, Barbara Donohoe Jostes Fund. Photo: Joseph McDonald.
2.39 Courtesy of Miyake Design Studio. Photo: Yasuaki Yoshinaga.
2.40 Fine Arts Museums of San Francisco, museum purchase, gift of Mr. and Mrs. Alfred S. Wilsey. Photo: Joseph McDonald.
2.41 Fine Arts Museums of San Francisco, Crown Point Press Archive, gift of Crown Point Press. Photo: Joseph McDonald.
2.42 Fine Arts Museums of San Francisco, Crown Point Press Archive, gift of Crown Point Press. Photo: Joseph McDonald.
2.43 Courtesy of Zandra Rhodes Publications U.S.A. Photo: Robyn Beeche.
2.44 Courtesy of Miyake Design Studio. Photo: Noriaki Yokosuka.
2.45 Courtesy Gemeentemuseum, Den Haag. Photo: Erik and Petra Hesmerg.
2.46 Courtesy of Alexandra Hart and Ann Funston. Photo: Jerry Wainwright.
2.47 Courtesy of *The New York Times*. Photo: Corina Lecca.
3.1 Courtesy of Ina Kozel.
3.2 Collection of the artist. Courtesy of Julie: Artisans' Gallery. Photo courtesy of Franko Khoury and Rebecca A. T. Stevens; photography by Franko Khoury.
3.3 Courtesy of Tim Harding. Photo: Petronella Ytsma.
3.4 Courtesy of Carter Smith.
3.5 Courtesy of Jacquelyn Roesch-Sanchez. Photo: Peter Mullett.
3.6 Courtesy of John Marshall.
3.7 Fine Arts Museums of San Francisco, gift of Wittenborn & Hollingsworth. Photo: Joseph McDonald.
3.8 Courtesy of Susie Hollingsworth. Photo: Tohru Nakamura.
3.9 Courtesy of Rose Kelly. Photo: Earl Fox.
3.10 Fine Arts Museums of San Francisco, gift of Bunny Horowitz. Photo: Joseph McDonald.
3.11 Courtesy of Susie Hollingsworth. Photo: Tohru Nakamura.
3.12 Courtesy of Estelle Akamine and Judy Reed. Photo: Judy Reed. Model: Corinne.
3.13 Courtesy of Ellen Hauptli. Photo: Elaine Keenan.
3.14 Courtesy of Jeanne Rose and Roger Mulkey. Photo: Roger Mulkey.
3.15 The Metropolitan Museum of Art, gift of Arthur and Joan Mahall and Family. Photo: ©1979 The Metropolitan Museum of Art.
3.16 Courtesy of Cat Chow.
3.17 Museum of Fine Arts, Boston, Daphne Farago Collection. Photo courtesy of Museum of Art, Rhode Island School of Design; photography by Del Bogart.
3.18 Fine Arts Museums of San Francisco, museum purchase, gift of Alma Kay Wong, the Textile Arts Council Endowment Fund, Marian Clayden, Peggy Gordon, Pamela Ransom, Santa Fe Weaving Gallery, Mr. and Mrs. Alfred S. Wilsey, Susan York, and various donors. Photo: Joseph McDonald.
3.19 Fine Arts Museums of San Francisco, museum purchase, Textile Arts Council Endowment Fund. Photo: Joseph McDonald.
3.20 Fine Arts Museums of San Francisco, gift of Mrs. John N. Rosekrans, Jr. Photo: Joseph McDonald.
3.21 The Garry and Sylvia Bennett Collection. Courtesy of Julie: Artisans' Gallery. Photo: Lee Fatherree.
3.22 Courtesy of Museum of Arts and Design. Photo: R. Jackson Smith.
3.23 Philadelphia Museum of Art, gift of Helen Williams Drutt English in honor of the artist, 2000. Courtesy of Philadelphia Museum of Art. Photo: Lynn Rosenthal.
3.24 Courtesy of Reina Mia Brill.
3.25 Courtesy of Arline Fisch. Photo: Will Gullette.
3.26 Courtesy of Randall Darwall. Photo: Morgan Rockhill.
3.27 Courtesy of Deborah Valoma. Photo: Lee Fatherree.
3.28 Fine Arts Museums of San Francisco, gift of Wittenborn and Hollingsworth. Photo: Joseph McDonald.
3.29 Courtesy of David and Erin Reese. Photo: David Reese.
3.30 Fine Arts Museums of San Francisco, museum purchase, gift of the Maggie Brosnan Memorial Fund. Photo courtesy of Candace Kling; photography by John Bagley.
3.31 Fine Arts Museums of San Francisco, gift of the artist. Photo: Joseph McDonald.
3.32 Fine Arts Museums of San Francisco, gift of the artist. Photo: Joseph McDonald.
3.33 Courtesy of Carol Lee Shanks. Photo: Don Tuttle.
3.34 Courtesy of Marian Clayden and Julie Schafler Dale, Custodian, Estate of Ben Compton. Photo: Roger Clayden.
3.35 Courtesy of Nancy Chappell. Photo: John Youngblood.
3.36 Courtesy of Janet Lipkin. Photo: Barry Shapiro.
3.37 Courtesy of Genevieve Dion.
3.38 Courtesy of the Fabric Workshop and Museum Staff.
3.39 Philadelphia Museum of Art, gift of Nancy McNeil. Photo courtesy of Philadelphia Museum of Art.
3.40 Collection of The Metropolitan Museum of Art, gift of Linda Mendelson. Photo: ©2004 The Metropolitan Museum of Art.
3.41 Courtesy of Susan Summa. Photo: R. Faller.
3.42 Collection of the artist. Courtesy of Julie: Artisans' Gallery. Photo courtesy of Susie Hollingsworth; photography by Tohru Nakamura.
3.43 Courtesy of Charlotte Kruk n' Kempken.
3.44 Courtesy of Frances Butler. Photo: Elaine Keenan.
3.45 Courtesy of Gaza Bowen. Photo: Michael Kirkpatrick.
3.46 Courtesy of Susie Hollingsworth. Photo: Tohru Nakamura.
3.47 Courtesy of Jean Williams Cacicedo. Photo: Barry Shapiro.
3.48 Courtesy of Yoshiko Wada. Photo: Joseph McDonald.
3.49 Fine Arts Museums of San Francisco, gift of Kenneth D. King. Photo: Joseph McDonald.
3.50 Fine Arts Museums of San Francisco, gift of the artist. Photo: Joseph McDonald.
4.1 Photo: David Scheinmann.
4.2 Courtesy of Susie Freeman. Photo: The Wellcome Trust.
4.3 Courtesy of Cameron Silver. Photo: Joseph McDonald.
4.4 Fine Arts Museums of San Francisco, gift of Diane K. Lloyd-Butler. Photo: Joseph McDonald.
4.5 Fine Arts Museums of San Francisco, gift of Diane K. Lloyd-Butler. Photo: Joseph McDonald.
4.6 Courtesy of the Helen Storey Foundation. Photo: Justine.
4.7 Courtesy of the Museum of Arts and Design. Photo: Eva Heyd.
4.8 Courtesy of the Museum of Arts and Design. Photo: Martin Tuma.
4.9 Courtesy of Susanna Heron. Photo: David Ward.
4.10 Courtesy of Arnoldsche. Photo: Katharina Thomas.
4.11 Courtesy of Arnoldsche.
4.12 Courtesy of Arnoldsche.
4.13 The Museum of Fine Arts, Houston; Helen Williams Drutt Collection. Photo courtesy of the Museum of Fine Arts, Houston.
4.14 Courtesy of Kent State University Museum. Photo: Anne Bissonnette.
4.15 Courtesy of Jorie Johnson. Photo: You Kobayashi.
4.16 Courtesy of Jane Harris. Photo: Shannon Tofts.
4.17 Courtesy of Mascha Mioni and Heiner Graafhuis. Photo: Asy Asendorf.
4.18 Courtesy of Walter Brix. Photo: Anne Gold.
4.19 Courtesy of Rolando Rasmussen.
4.20 Courtesy of Ellen Eis. Photo Rolf Brauneis.
4.21 Courtesy of the Museum of Arts and Design. Photo: Eva Heyd.
4.22 From *Brahaus* by Samuele Mazza ©1994. Granted with permission from Chronicle Books LLC. Visit ChronicleBooks.com
4.23 Courtesy of Jenny Kee, Greg Barrett, and The Powerhouse Museum of Applied Arts and Sciences. Photo: Greg Barrett/AC.
4.24 Courtesy of Barbara Rogers. Photo: Warwick Clarke.
4.25 Courtesy of The Powerhouse Museum of Applied Arts and Sciences and Stephen Galloway. Photo: Monty Coles.
4.26 Courtesy of Shin Young-ok.
4.27 Courtesy of The Montana World of Wearable Art Awards. Photo: Craig Potton.
4.28 Courtesy of Craig Potton Publishing, Ltd. Photo: Craig Potton.
4.29 Courtesy of The Korea Fashion & Culture Association. Photo: Lee Hyui Sae.
4.30 Courtesy of The Korea Fashion & Culture Association. Photo: Lee Hyui Sae.
4.31 Courtesy of The Korea Fashion & Culture Association. Photo: Lee Hyui Sae.
4.32 Courtesy of the Museum of Arts and Design. Photo: Eva Heyd.
4.33 Courtesy of Chunghie Lee.
4.34 Courtesy of Yoko Ishigaki. Photo: Makoto Yano.
4.35 Courtesy of Suzumi Noda. Photo: Syuzo Ogushi.
4.36 Courtesy of Noriko Narahira.
4.37 Courtesy of Jorie Johnson. Photo: You Kobayashi.
5.1 Courtesy of Estelle Akamine. Photo: David Vernali.
5.2 Fine Arts Museums of San Francisco, museum purchase, gift of Alma Kay Wong, Textile Arts Council Endowment Fund, Marian Clayden, Peggy Gordon, Pamela Ransom, Santa Fe Weaving Gallery, Mr. and Mrs. Alfred S. Wilsey, Susan York, and various donors. Photo: Joseph McDonald.
5.3 Courtesy of Debra Rapoport. Photo: Demetre Lagios.
5.4 Courtesy of Mary Griffin. Photo: Roger Schreiber.
5.5 Courtesy of Diana Aurigemma. Photo: Roger Schreiber.
5.6 Courtesy of Roger Schreiber. Photo: Roger Schreiber.
5.7 Fine Arts Museums of San Francisco, museum purchase, gift of Alma Kay Wong, Textile Arts Council Endowment Fund, Marian Clayden, Peggy Gordon, Pamela Ransom, Santa Fe Weaving Gallery, Mr. and Mrs. Alfred S. Wilsey, Susan York, and various donors.
5.8 Courtesy of Robert Kushner.
5.9 Courtesy of Nick Cave. Photo: Stephen Hamilton.
5.10 Courtesy of Nick Cave. Photo: Stephen Hamilton.
5.11 Courtesy of Robert Kushner. Photo: Harry Shunk.
5.12 Courtesy of Pat Oleszko. Photo: Neil Selkirk.
5.13 Courtesy of Pat Oleszko. Photo: Neil Selkirk.
5.14 Courtesy of Copia: The American Center for Wine, Food, and the Arts. Photo: Kaz Tsuruta.
5.15 Courtesy of the Fabric Workshop and Museum Staff.
5.16 Fine Arts Museums of San Francisco, gift of Louise Allrich. Photo: Joseph McDonald.
5.17 Fine Arts Museums of San Francisco, gift of the artist. Photo courtesy of Yvonne Porcella; photography by Sharon Risedorph.
5.18 Courtesy of Tim Harding. Photo: Petronella Ytsma.
5.19 Courtesy of Marian Schoettle. Photo: Will Faller.
5.20 Courtesy of Helen Drutt English.
5.21 Fine Arts Museums of San Francisco, museum purchase, Barbara Donohoe Jostes Bequest Fund. Photo: Joseph McDonald.
5.22 Fine Arts Museums of San Francisco, museum purchase, gift of the Textile Arts Council. Photo courtesy of Gaza Bowen; photography by Michael Kirkpatrick
5.23 Courtesy of Caroline Broadhead/Barrett Marsden Gallery. Photo: David Ward.
5.24 Courtesy of Thames & Hudson.
5.25 Courtesy of Marian Schoettle. Photo: Marian Schoettle.
5.26 Courtesy of the Fabric Workshop and Museum. Photo: Marion Boulton Stroud.
5.27 Fine Arts Museums of San Francisco, museum purchase, Barbara Donohoe Jostes Fund. Photo: Joseph McDonald.
5.28 Courtesy of Jon Eric Riis. Photo: Barts' Art, Atlanta.
5.29 Sweet Briar College Pannell Art Gallery Collection, gift of Jane Roseberry Tolleson. Photo: Charles Grubbs.
5.30 Photo: Marian Schoettle.
5.31 Courtesy of Carol Lee Shanks. Photo: Don Tuttle.
5.32 Spencer Museum of Art, University of Kansas, museum purchase. Photo courtesy of Spencer Museum of Art, University of Kansas.
5.33 Courtesy of Christine LoFaso. Photo: Jerry Kobylecky.
5.34 Courtesy of Franko Khoury and Rebecca A. T. Stevens. Photo: Franko Khoury.
5.35 Courtesy of Arnoldsche.
5.36 Courtesy of Robert Hillestad. Photo: John Nollendorfs.

Index